ENCODING **SPACE**

SHAPING LEARNING ENVIRONMENTS THAT UNLOCK HUMAN POTENTIAL

Brian Mathews & Leigh Ann Soistmann

The paper used in this publication meets the minimum requirements of American National Standard for Information Sciences–Permanence of Paper for Printed Library Materials, ANSI Z39.48-1992. ∞

Library of Congress Cataloging-in-Publication Data

Names: Mathews, Brian (Brian Scott), author | Soistmann, Leigh Ann, author.
Title: Encoding space : shaping learning environments that unlock human
    potential / by Brian Mathews and Leigh Ann Soistmann.
Description: Chicago : Association of College and Research Libraries, a
    division of the American Library Association, 2016.
Identifiers: LCCN 2015047985 | ISBN 9780838988251 (pbk. : alk. paper)
Subjects: LCSH: Libraries--Space utilization. | Academic libraries--Space
    utilization. | Academic libraries--Planning. | Library
    buildings--Psychological aspects. | Architecture--Psychological aspects.
Classification: LCC Z679.55 .M38 2016 | DDC 022/.9--dc23 LC record available at http://lccn.loc.
gov/2015047985

Printed in the United States of America.

20 19 18 17 16   5 4 3 2 1

DEDICATION

To Anne M. Mulheron, Mr. Lowe, and others who aspire to improve library experiences.

"Anne M. Mulheron described the new branch of the Portland, Oregon, Library Association, in which a definite plan has been followed to make the library as homelike as possible. To supplement the plan in this attempt at homelikeness, wicker chairs, floor reading lamps, draperies of monk's cloth, rugs, pictures, and shelving painted in bright color, have been introduced into the furnishings.

It was pointed out that it was only so short a time ago as the Saratoga Springs meeting that these very ideas advocated by Mr. Lowe had been greeted with laughter and contempt, in spite of the fact that he was reporting their successful adaptation in so unpromising surroundings as an army cantonment library."

Papers and Proceedings of the Forty-Eighth Annual Meeting. Bulletin of the American Library Association, October 1926, 521-525.

A STEP FORWARD

THIS BOOK IS INTENDED TO BE A CONVERSATION STARTER.

I've gathered an assortment of observations, stories, experiments, renderings, and sketches to inspire discussion about the future purpose of library buildings. Over the past decade, library interiors have undergone some radical changes, and my intention is to encourage us to take the next step forward and ask: What might libraries become?

The ideas presented here are not meant to be prescriptive. In fact, I prefer to think of this as the beginning of a visioning session. These pages are filled with many questions and tangents. My hope is that Encoding Spaces will ignite your imagination and offer guidance through some thought-provoking concepts to reflect on and further explore within the context of your learning environment.

Brian Mathews
December 2015

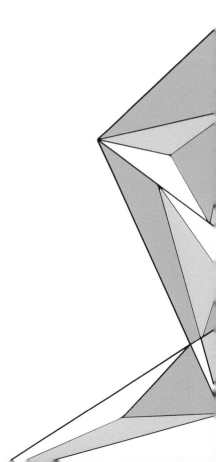

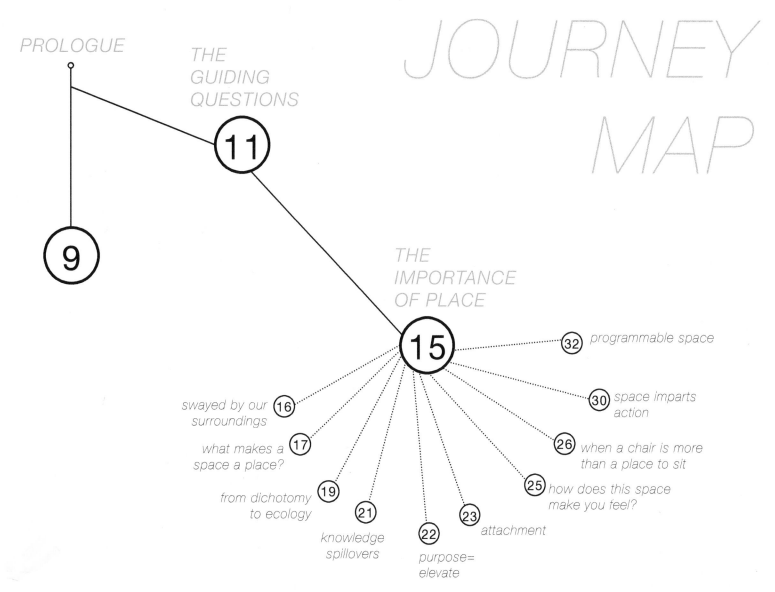

PROLOGUE

THE
GUIDING
QUESTIONS

JOURNEY

MAP

11

9

THE
IMPORTANCE
OF PLACE

15

32 programmable space

30 space imparts
action

16 swayed by our
surroundings

26 when a chair is more
than a place to sit

17 what makes a
space a place?

25 how does this space
make you feel?

19 from dichotomy
to ecology

21

23 attachment

22

knowledge
spillovers

purpose=
elevate

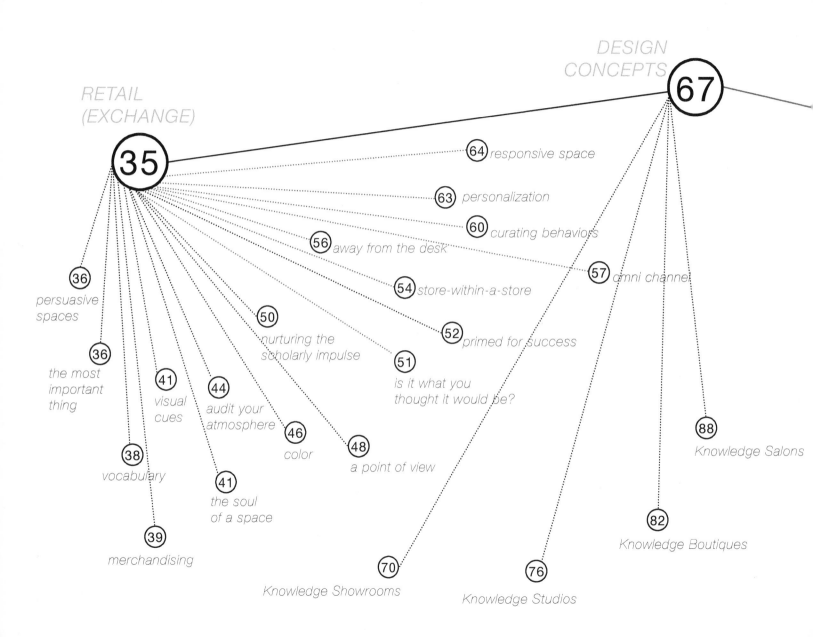

RETAIL
(EXCHANGE)

35

DESIGN
CONCEPTS

67

64 responsive space

63 personalization

60 curating behaviors

56 away from the desk

57 omni channel

54 store-within-a-store

52 primed for success

50

nurturing the
scholarly impulse

51

is it what you
thought it would be?

36

persuasive
spaces

36

the most
important
thing

41

visual
cues

44

audit your
atmosphere

46

color

48

a point of view

38

vocabulary

41

the soul
of a space

39

merchandising

70

Knowledge Showrooms

76

Knowledge Studios

82

Knowledge Boutiques

88

Knowledge Salons

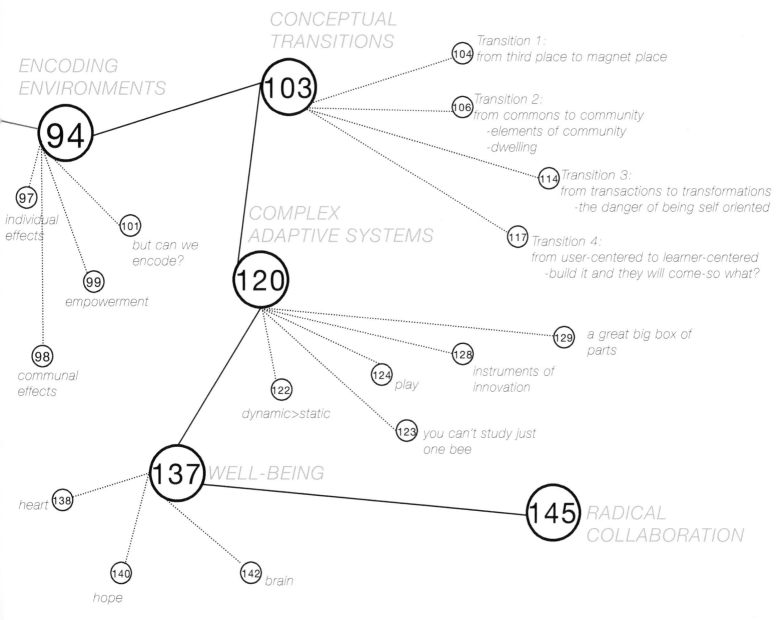

ENCODING
ENVIRONMENTS

CONCEPTUAL
TRANSITIONS

94

103

104 Transition 1:
from third place to magnet place

106 Transition 2:
from commons to community
-elements of community
-dwelling

114 Transition 3:
from transactions to transformations
-the danger of being self oriented

117 Transition 4:
from user-centered to learner-centered
-build it and they will come-so what?

97
individual
effects

101
but can we
encode?

99
empowerment

98
communal
effects

COMPLEX
ADAPTIVE SYSTEMS

120

129 a great big box of
parts

128 instruments of
innovation

124 play

122
dynamic>static

123 you can't study just
one bee

137 WELL-BEING

heart 138

145 RADICAL
COLLABORATION

140
hope

142 brain

7

PROLOGUE

WHAT'S THE BUILDING TRYING TO TELL US?

Space transmits culture. It conveys the body language of an organization. Our buildings may be inanimate, but they are not inarticulate. A neglected structure makes a clear statement, just as much as a beautiful one does. It sends a message about priorities.

Buildings, especially libraries, are symbolic. They represent the intellectual character and aspirations of a college, university, or community. The condition of these facilities speaks volumes about what is valued.

BUILDINGS COMMUNICATE WITH US.

ARE WE LISTENING?

THE GUIDING QUESTIONS

Can we create environments that inspire people to be more creative, collaborative, reflective, or engaged?

As libraries shape-shift in response to digital migration and other seismic changes, our spaces have emerged as experimental landscapes fostering personal growth and multimodal expression. Our buildings are active laboratories for human progress.

Our goal is to create opportunities for people to engage with multiple streams of information and data and to interact with each other in new and different ways. We want them to learn to break down complex problems and transfer skills, tools, concepts, and mind-sets across many different situations.

As we glance to the future, a number of questions must be explored in terms of how we develop, manage, and conceive of library spaces.

What are our intentions? What are the intentions of our users? Are they the same or different?

Who is our primary audience? What other groups and stakeholders do we need to consider?

What impact does the arrangement of furniture and technology have on what can be accomplished? What mood does it create?

What does the design and condition of the library facility say about our institution?

Does one's relationship with a building factor into personal success?

Do perceptions influence outcomes? Do outcomes, in turn, affect perceptions?

And perhaps the ultimate question:

Can physical space unlock greater human potential?

I ask that you keep an open mind on this journey as we dive into some uncharted waters and imagine what a library facility can become. These pages may challenge some of our long-held beliefs and assumptions, but I think that is a necessary activity in order to stimulate our thinking to forge ahead in the decades to come.

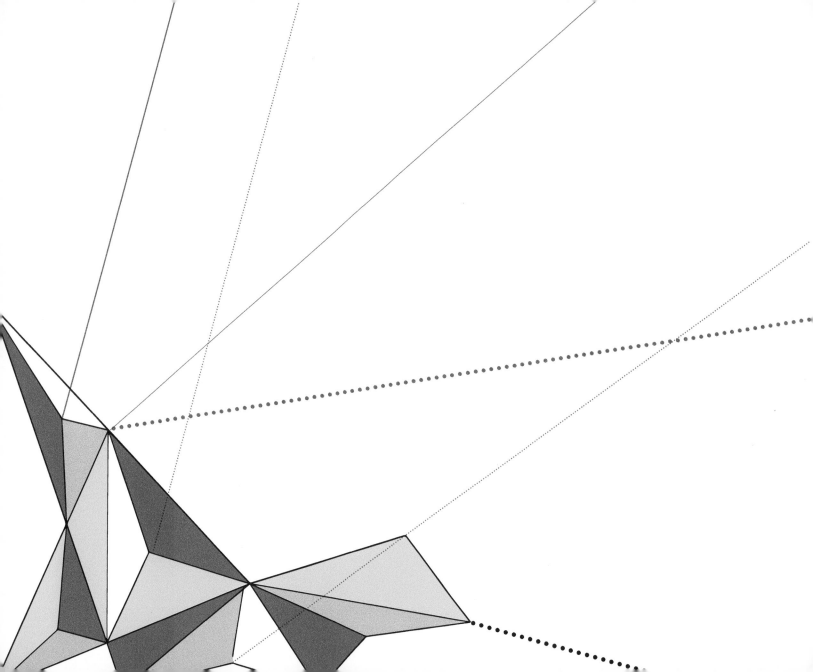

THE IMPORTANCE
OF PLACE

Swayed By Our Surroundings

In 1956 Abraham Maslow published a seminal paper on the influence our physical surroundings have on us. Participants viewed photographs of people's faces and evaluated them based on different attributes. Maslow wanted to test how people reacted to the content while located in different physical environments. Some viewed the images while seated in a beautiful office, while others did so in a grungy janitor's closet. In the nice room, people looking at the photos saw faces filled with energy and well-being. These same faces were rated as fatigued and sickly when viewed in the run-down room. Maslow surmised that the condition of our surroundings has an impact on not only our emotions, but our judgment as well.

This concept appears repeatedly across many disciplines. Various studies support the notion that space affects our mood and behaviors. From architects and interior designers, to psychologists and neuroscientists, to community developers and retail managers, one finds numerous accounts of how physical environments have an impact on the way we think, feel, learn, and act.

We each respond consciously (and often unconsciously) to the places where we live, work, hang out, or otherwise visit or inhabit throughout our day. These spaces influence what we get done, whom we engage with, and how we interact with the world around us. In fact, the places where we spend the most of our time affect who we are and what we can become. *Space shapes us just as much as we shape it.*

Reading more about the psychological and philosophical nature of space has changed my approach to planning library environments. We have to keep in mind that our efforts are not just about form, function, and efficiency. Our decisions have a direct impact on the cognitive growth and well-being of our communities.

Librarians are increasingly allocating more of their building's physical footprint for classrooms, commons areas, and specialized studios. This change affords us many opportunities for engagement but also a tremendous responsibility. More people are using our services and facilities in different ways; they are counting on us. But I think we are imparting something deeper: We're influencing how people think and feel about learning, research, knowledge, and themselves.

Studies suggest that the quality of the learning environment has a great effect on the quality of the learning that happens there. From test scores, to attendance, to class participation, the character of the building is a significant predictor of success. This finding extends further than academic achievement and also correlates with feelings of self-esteem and confidence.

When students feel safe, valued, and taken care of, it gives them a great advantage. We can't ignore this. The condition of our libraries expresses far more than our reverence for the preservation of knowledge or academic success; the condition of our libraries is directly aligned with personal, social, and intellectual advancement of our communities.

What Makes A Space A Place?

We are increasingly expanding the spectrum of services in our buildings. From makerspaces and visualization labs to digital scholarship centers and design studios, the library landscape is changing rapidly and radically.

But there is one thing we can't design: a sense of place.

There is much debate about what constitutes a "place" and how it is different from a "space." And after poring through pages on the topic, it seems that a space becomes a place when it rises above being a mere utility. Places have social and personal significance. They mean something to us. We get drawn in and emotionally invested by what we can do there and by how it makes us feel. It is through this process of accruing experiences that a space transforms into a place.

Think about it like this: Imagine a coffee shop that you like and visit frequently. How is it different from similar establishments? Do you look forward to going there? Do you feel happy afterward? That's the basic difference between being in a space (any random coffee shop) and being in a place (your favorite coffee shop).

Spaces also become places when they take on cultural significance. Here is an example: there is an interesting account of two scientists visiting an old castle. From a rational perspective, the castle is just an assortment of bricks, wood, and metal that has stood for centuries. In fact, Europe is littered with many structures just like it. But when it is revealed to be Kronborg, the mythical home of Shakespeare's Hamlet, their perspective changes. The pile of bricks is now imbued with mystery, romance, intrigue, and sorrow. Just being there incites certain emotions and a sense of awe and wonder.

Why is this important? As we reimagine libraries, I think we want to create opportunities for people to bond with and within our environments. Historically we have been able to point to the rows of stacks and talk about libraries as sacred places because of the collections. But that seems to be changing.

If all we are providing is a place to study or a computer lab for work on assignments, then that doesn't particularly require a library. As we face a future with fewer print materials, what components and aspects can elevate us from just another space into a place that is a significant part of the learning and research journey?

From Dichotomy To Ecology

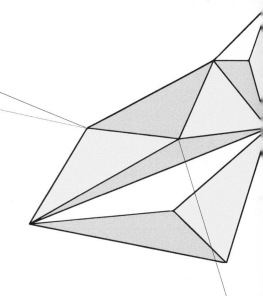

Is the dominant personality of libraries shifting from introverted to extroverted? Can we posit that libraries in the past catered to the lone scholar: an individual working independently, largely in solitude?

And now, alongside the growth of the Web, the emergence of mobile technologies, and an evolving curriculum that encourages teamwork, we can trace a shift in the character of our spaces. Not only are we seeing more people using libraries overall, but perhaps we're also attracting people who would not have used our buildings in the past. We're not only adding more people space, we're also adding new types of spaces that alter the social dynamic.

It's understandable how this sea change can induce confusion, concern, and dismay, particularly among faculty. While some feed off the energy in our commons areas and are thrilled to see students so engaged, others feel it is wasteful and a poor investment of library space.

Likewise with students: Some may express positive feedback and become frequent users, while others grumble about their seemingly endless quest to find silent study nooks.

I'm wondering, though, how much of this tension boils down to one's personality or temperament? Does our bias blind us, blocking us from recognizing other people's preferences?

We may currently find ourselves facing a clash between quiet versus collaborative spaces. But perhaps we can look at this differently? Instead, what if we looked at library environments as an ecology: a wide spectrum of people working in parallel on different objectives?

Let's think of people as hybrid users who flow in and out of different work modes. Instead of creating user categories, what if we look at this as a seamless process? Rather than pigeonholing people as introverts and extroverts, let's consider their project journey. In some cases, students will need to meet and mingle with their peers and classmates. But then they might break away to think, continue solo work, or mentally rejuvenate themselves. Certain parts of assignments may be ideal for high-energy, high-interaction locations, while others work better in a more subdued setting. Just as some portions of a project may require sharing, debating, and concept mapping, other parts demand extra reflection and concentration.

Can we make this ebb and flow as continuous as possible? Let's aim to enable our students to move about and change what's around them based on their mood or the current status of their work. In this manner, we're not building a collection of independent spaces, but rather a rich, interrelated, and harmonious landscape.

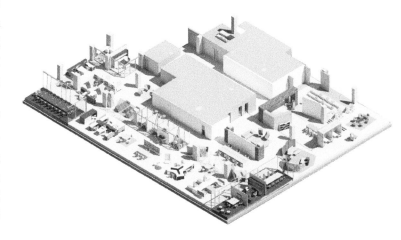

Knowledge Spillovers

Another important component of place is the people who inhabit it. Research suggests that sharing knowledge and skills through formal and informal interaction generates significant knowledge spillovers. A tool from one discipline might unlock new possibilities when applied to a different domain. Or an insight generated in one area brings a new context to another.

When people are clustered together, they share ideas or look at problems and potential in different ways. This ecosystem of serendipity can lead to breakthroughs, innovations, and novel developments.

How can libraries build a vibrant culture where knowledge and skills are exchanged and showcased? While we have long offered open collections that promote discovery and exposure, what if we designed our spaces specifically for cross-fertilization and chance encounters?

artists-in-residence working beside scientists-in-residence

fashion design students sharing their creative processes with interior design majors and digital media developers

studios next to labs next to commons areas next to cafes next to galleries next to whiteboards next to large digital displays

Wrapped in this landscape are various support services (writing, media production, literacies, tech help) that encourage exploration and celebrate experiments. And further nestled within this high-sensory environment are mental buffers for meditative and solitary work.

This knowledge ecosystem is based upon the life cycle of learning. Just as it propels interaction and collaboration (what if we tried this), it also supports the need to retreat, reflect, and internalize (space to hear yourself think) before starting the process over again.

Purpose = Elevate

Libraries are destinations that people choose to visit. Their reasons and needs may be different each time they walk through the doors, or even shift over the course a day.

Why do they come in?
What are they doing?
What's holding them back?
What's moving them forward?

Librarians have long been stewards of the historical record. Our professional DNA is hardwired to collect, protect, and disseminate information. We create order from chaos. We make things findable. We help people discover content. We encourage them to read. We support critical analysis. This is what we do.

But things are changing, or rather, expanding. I increasingly hear library leaders talking about moving from being focused on information consumption to a more encompassing role facilitating knowledge production. Let's ponder that. What does this mean for our collections? What does a dematerializing library look like? And how does this influence the way our buildings get used and perceived, and the impact it has on what people are trying to accomplish? Or put differently: What are we ourselves trying to accomplish through the design and provision of our facilities?

As we introduce new programs and services, our aspirations are entwined with the idea of empowerment. We encourage people to make things, design ideas, test concepts, and push themselves (and their thoughts) in new directions. Today we are focused on the fusion of knowledge practices.

While we obviously promote productivity and inquiry, do we ever pause and wonder if people are happy? Let me be clear; I'm not talking about satisfied with the performance of library operations or delighted by good customer service. Instead: What if our spaces could actually elevate an emotional state? What if the arrangement of a commons area could alter someone's mood? What if we could create environments that generate a sense of joyfulness and intellectual purpose? This is the way I think about library spaces.

Librarians are a pragmatic bunch, and we spend much of our time focused on functionality. We're utilitarian by default. Ours is a world of constraints: unpredictable financial resources combined with limited physical footprints, surrounded by ever-changing technology and placed within hierarchical organizational structures, all while trying to support diverse user populations with varied needs and expectations.

So what's our purpose? Libraries are more than just a place to read. And for that matter, they are more than just a place to create knowledge. They represent something greater than the sum of editing essays, writing code, designing graphics, rehearsing presentations, calculating proofs, solving problems, or brainstorming ideas. A well-crafted space moves us beyond utility. Libraries are truly significant when their value extends beyond the outputs they enable.

Attachment

If we want to elevate the way people feel when they use the library, then we need to elevate the way they feel about the library itself. We need to create environments that stimulate an emotional connection.

So what aspects help foster a sense of place?

It's not the cutting-edge technology or designer furniture. It's not large windows with panoramic views. Nor is it an enormous print collection, a café, or great customer service. And despite what students might tell you, it's not ample table space to spread out with robust wireless access and plenty of power outlets.

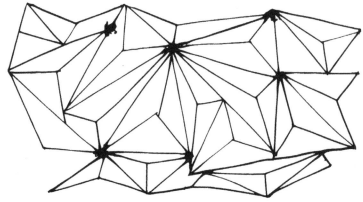

So what is it then? The answer might surprise you. When community developers explored attributes pertaining to place attachment, they found that the best predictor is a strong social tie. When measuring sentiment, it wasn't the age or condition of the homes, high-quality parks and schools, or any other amenities. It was actually the relationships with people around them. Apparently, the more connected we feel with our neighbors, the better we feel about our neighborhood and our place within it. Even people who are more introverted had a greater sense of attachment if they had had positive interactions with those around them.

This sentiment is echoed in other studies. For instance, social bonding between hikers and other recreationists is the strongest indicator of attachment to certain parks. While hikers may enjoy challenging trails and natural beauty, many are also seeking interpersonal opportunities and want to share the experience with friends and family.

Studies also suggest that students who participate in living-learning residential communities, as opposed to dorms, perform better academically. They also have an easier time transitioning into college and tend to develop a greater attachment to the institution.

While some students and faculty may seek out the library as a place of solitude, the fact is that they are doing so among others who value that same condition. Even if you prefer to be tucked away behind the stacks, others around you are also silent and respectful of this shared desire. It's a community of the quiet people. This would be different, though, if someone seeking silence encountered a neighbor who was loud and disruptive. The people around us have a huge impact on how we feel about our environments.

We become attached to places because of what they enable us to do. They can provide us with energy and support and supply us with inspiration and comfort. These places enhance our lives on a continuing basis. If we want students and others to feel this way about libraries, then they need the ability to participate, adapt, and appropriate the surroundings accordingly.

A place (rather than a space) encourages students to be active residents who define, interpret, search, and modify the settings for achieving personal goals. Whether it is a quiet nook or a high-energy collaboration hub doesn't really matter. What does matter is feeling a sense of ownership and camaraderie that elevates the experience.

How Does This Space Make You Feel?

Libraries have certain noises. The soundscape, ranging from intense concentration to lively collaboration, is unparalleled. Even our quiet reading rooms have a particular hum—the energy of people surrounded by other like-minded people reading, typing, thinking, and dreaming. Our buildings host a symphony that is performed daily by our visitors.

I've spent years trying to improve the harmony. How can I help people work better?

The most valuable insights I've encountered have come from sharing space with the students themselves. To understand their situation, I had to experience it firsthand. I needed to work where they worked. See what they saw. And feel what they felt. I needed to inhabit the environment alongside them. So I frequently take my own work out into the commons landscape.

Over time you recognize a choreography in how a space ebbs and flows between calm and frenetic. You realize that certain people can completely alter the demeanor of a room. Or you watch with interest when one group leaves and another sets up camp. As a space designer, you start asking questions that otherwise would have remained invisible.

In my conversations with library residents, I've repeatedly encountered stories from groups and individuals about being able to get things done. It seems there is a psychological alchemy that occurs once people walk through our doors. Visiting a library unlocks certain mental modes, different ways of thinking, seeing, and being.

Students and faculty leave our buildings with a sense of accomplishment. A trip to the library is an investment in self-improvement.

WHEN A CHAIR IS MORE
THAN A PLACE TO SIT

I vividly recall a particular conversation with a student team that expanded my thoughts on commons areas. They felt that they could write code together better when working in the library. I probed for more details. They admitted that using their laptops enabled them to work from anywhere, but the library presented them with a unique combination of features. The mixture of physical, technological, social, and aesthetic components propelled their work. The group also noted that they always run into old friends or encounter people they don't see regularly in their classes or residential areas. The value proposition for them is being able to share, move, create, test, and bond in ways they couldn't achieve elsewhere.

This communal aspect is intriguing. People are not coming to libraries only to get work done; they also want an audience and to be part of the performance. They position themselves around other people who are working on their own assignments. *We're all in this together.* It's a shared effort. Being surrounded by other productive people is a powerful motivator.

I've since noticed related activities. For example, when given an opportunity, many students will alter furniture to meet their needs. They might move a table near a window or drag a chair next to a friend. Some will adjust lamps, window shades, or portable partitions. This idea of modifying a room to address immediate needs serves both functional and emotional desires. And it's a key element for encoding space. Our message to them: *Make it your own.*

Some students feel better sitting a particular way in a particular chair in a particular place at a particular time. In essence, a chair is more than just a place to sit; it is an instrumental part of the larger ecosystem and has a direct impact on the pursuit of learning.

Places enhance our moods and affect the way we feel about the activities we are doing. As Maslow suggested with his room study, an uncomfortable environment makes working on projects feel more laborious, whereas an inspiring environment uplifts the spirit bringing about greater results. As learning space developers, we have to recognize that architecture is more than just a building filled with furnishings; it is a way to influence the thoughts and feelings of those inside.

Spaces need to be flexible because the user identity keeps changing:

listener, planner, arguer, designer, coder, thinker, writer, and presenter.

Space Imparts Action

Imagine you are teaching in a classroom filled with rows of desktop computers. What impact does this arrangement have on your approach? Now imagine that you are in a room outfitted with movable furniture, portable whiteboards, and a cart of laptops. Would you teach differently?

One setup isn't necessarily better than the other; they both enable different things to happen. If you are demonstrating software and want people to follow along, then the fixed room would be suitable. If you want students to move about and interact in small groups, then the flexible arrangement is more ideal.

The space has an impact on what we can do within it.

You've probably experienced this during meetings. A room's circular setup creates a different dynamic than one featuring a long rectangular table. The configuration of the furniture affects the way people engage with each other and the manner that topics are discussed. There is a big difference between sharing information and shaping it together.

Kurt Lewin, a seminal social psychologist, explored this idea eighty years ago. He expressed it as a formula:

$$B = F(P, E)$$

Essentially, behavior is a function of a person (or group) and his or her immediate environment. The way the room is arranged has an impact on how people learn, what they can do, and how they feel.

What behaviors are you trying to encourage in your building?

How does the environment help or hinder those intentions?

Introducing new furniture or technology will influence how a space is used and by whom. A noisy group entering a quiet area will alter the dynamic of the room. Desktop computers with two chairs beside them can encourage collaborative work. Seating arrangements influence associations. Our job, then, is to think about the wide array of interactions (behaviors) that we want to support and then to develop spaces that encourage those outcomes.

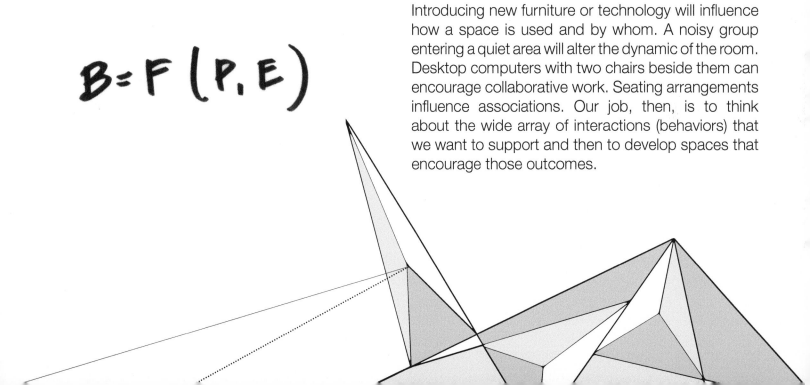

Programmable Space

One of the most valuable ways to think about physical space is to compare it with virtual space. If you manage a website, there are things you can do to influence how it is used, from selecting certain colors, fonts, and graphics to presenting content, navigation, and interactive components. An information architecture works behind the scenes to bring it all together.

Analytics, usability testing, and other tools allow you to monitor the actions occurring across your pages. You can change settings to make it better: Rename links, resize images, move text, or place greater emphasis on certain areas. By modifying the code, you modify the virtual environment and ultimately how people experience your web presence. Changing the environment influences people's behaviors.

I view library buildings in the same manner: It is all programmable space. We can move book stacks, computers, or study carrels and arrange them differently. We can introduce temporary features such as exhibits, installations, or events.

We can optimize certain areas depending on how they are framed and where they are located throughout our buildings. We can alter the experience (and behaviors) by altering the environment.

An idea that sparked my imagination was a series of experiments conducted in school cafeterias. Researchers found that they could influence student's food selection simply by arranging the choices in different ways. For example, it is possible to increase healthy eating by emphasizing certain foods and deemphasizing others, even when the same inventory is available. What really mattered was how the food was presented and when the decision was compelled as students moved through the line. Easy access to healthy food early on was the critical factor.

This is a powerful concept. It encourages us to think of ourselves as *choice architects*, not just learning space managers. A library building presents visitors with many choices, and they have to make a series of decisions about what they need for the task at hand. We are presenting them with a physical interface. As they navigate through our spaces, they are exposed to many different possibilities. Our task is to apply the principles of usability and offer intuitive options. In this manner we become interaction designers, creating a diverse range of settings for a variety of intended outcomes.

RETAIL
EXCHANGE

Persuasive Spaces

As I've evolved as a learning space developer, I've found myself increasingly drawn to retail environments. On a basic level, stores serve as browsable warehouses, where people move through a space and are exposed to many different items. The merchant hopes to make transactions and a profit—but there is more to it than that. The core purpose of a marketplace is to facilitate an exchange. This concept of trade is intriguing since people use libraries to find, share, and develop ideas, tools, skills, and knowledge.

Move beyond the service-oriented perspective, and these spaces take on a different shape. Stores are "theatres of consumption" that seek to "tantalize the imagination" and offer settings that "inspire, encourage, and reassure." Retail environments are programmed to persuade and to make us feel, act, and think in certain ways. I'm fascinated with the idea that simply being in a store could make me feel happy, sociable, or reflective and, of course, make me want to buy something that I didn't realize I needed.

Manipulative? Perhaps. But we can learn from this example. Since the environment has a direct impact on behaviors and emotions, it behooves us to study the science and tactics of merchandising so that we can curate powerful places as well. Concepts adapted from retail can help us build better libraries: spaces that emote knowledge, learning, creativity, or whatever other attributes we want to portray.

If the spaces that we inhabit affect what we do and how we feel, then our challenge is to create environments that enable people to recognize their potential and to become better versions of themselves.

The Most Important Thing

If you look through the literature on retail environments, a universal truth emerges: *you need to make people feel good.* Research suggests that customers typically spend more money when they are in a positive mood. In fact, when they are enjoying the experience, they spend more time browsing and interacting with a larger amount of inventory. Hence, a key design objective of merchants is exposing customers to more of what is available. By instilling a sense of curiosity and comfort, shopping transforms from a mundane chore into a more fulfilling activity.

Happy customers have a higher probability of realizing their purchase goals and, therefore, feeling a sense of achievement. This perception of success feeds into their sense of satisfaction with the store but also with themselves. Smart shoppers are the ones who feel they chose the right place to accomplish their purpose.

This theme applies in other domains as well. For instance, research suggests that patients heal faster when they are in environments that reduce stress. Hospitals seek to support this through designs that provide patients with a sense of control, positive distraction, and possibilities of social support. The fear of the unknown is very apparent in medical settings, so by providing people with a feeling of influence over certain conditions in their rooms, hospitals can ensure their patients feel more comfortable and eased.

This concept of happiness is evident in how libraries have evolved over the recent decades. We've moved from banning all food and drinks to opening cafés. Our furniture has changed from institutionalized aesthetics to more attractive options.

Generally speaking, as information sources have become more digitally abundant, we have started converting library spaces into environments that are more appealing.

But perhaps the most revolutionary advancement has been the burst of outreach. Activities such as game nights, dog-petting programs, makerspace competitions, poetry readings, diversity and inclusion events, stress-relieving activities, and free food during finals are reshaping the personality of our organizations. At the core, we want students and others to feel welcomed and comfortable. We want them lingering and spending longer periods of time inhabiting in our spaces. We want them to explore our services, virtually and physically, and to be exposed to our wide spectrum of offerings. These principles are very similar to those of a good retailer.

While we strive to help people to be productive, we should also aim to ensure they feel good about their effort as well. We want people to leave the library in a positive mood—with a sense of confidence and accomplishment. Every trip to our buildings represents an opportunity for personal advancement.

So how do we develop these mood-altering spaces? Let's take a closer look at interior design principles for some guidance.

Vocabulary

The world of interior design is immense and complicated. It truly is a science and an art. As librarians assume greater responsibility in managing active physical environments and shaping interactions, it benefits us to learn the language.

Here are some basics to get us started:

Harmony - the sense that everything belongs together. The room arrangement blends furniture and design elements (colors, shapes, sizes) into a unified concept.

Contrast – the arrangement of opposing elements (light vs. dark colors, patterns vs. solids, hard vs. smooth textures, large vs. small shapes, etc.) to create visual interest.

Balance – the visual weight of the room. The composition of elements creates an impression of equilibrium or symmetry.

Rhythm – the visual flow, or the movement of the eye across a space.

Repetition – the recurrence of features throughout a space such as the same color, pattern, texture, or furniture element.

Emphasis - focal points or visual centers of attraction within a room.

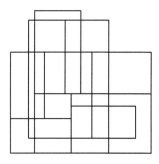

As you become familiar with these concepts, you begin to see differently. I often notice when things look out of place or how color guides my eye throughout a room. Additionally, when all of the furniture is identical, it blends together, whereas tables with different shapes, heights, and color help define the layout. And yet, too much variety throws things off balance.

Not only do you have to consider the functional intention of your spaces, but you have to consider the emotional intention as well. If a room is too busy, it can create a mental fatigue, while too empty a space could dampen the spirit.

There isn't a single blueprint for success. A space for high-energy group collaboration requires a different setting from one for individuals concentrating alone, just as the ideal space for brainstorming is different from one for composition, coding, or presentation rehearsal. We know that the environment shapes human action, so start by defining what you want to enable people to do (the behaviors). Then craft a space that communicates those objectives.

Merchandising

While the environments we create might be harmonious, exciting, soothing, or aesthetically pleasing, we must keep their purpose in mind. Spaces should have intentionality. In retail the floor plans and various displays are meant to stimulate sales. We can deploy similar tactics to encourage a different set of outcomes.

Visual merchandising involves a store's overall presentation: the layout. It entices us to explore. It piques our curiosity, sustains our interest, and causes us to linger—and to keep coming back. It is a form of storytelling that highlights potential and introduces us to new ideas.

Bakeries serve as a great case study. Their inventory is carefully displayed and curated in an appealing manner. The smells trigger our desire. The arrangement of breads, cookies, and pastries is alluring. The items are small luxuries in themselves, iced and decorated to resemble gifts: *Treat yourself.* We might even enjoy a free sample to help persuade us. Simply entering the space activates our senses.

How might we apply this effect in libraries? My circulation team experimented by placing lending technology in full view. Previously, adaptors and other equipment were stored in a back room. Moving it out front made it more visible and increased borrowing. This not only made it easier for students to point directly to what they wanted, but it also ignited conversations about the accessories and suggestions for other gadgets that would be helpful.

Visual merchandising concepts can be applied widely across commons areas. For example, showcasing the output from 3-D printers can generate more awareness of and desirability for these types of tools. Relevant information, such as printing costs and time requirements, could be attached to various models. This approach allows us to stimulate interest while managing expectations. Similarly, displays on a visualization wall not only showcase content, but also can communicate the idea that libraries are places with multimedia tools and experts. Our message becomes *you can build stuff like this here.*

By incorporating merchandising tactics inspired by retailers, we can visually articulate the intention of our environments. As students and others move through our buildings, we can offer them an interactive menu of choices, empowering them to address their needs and recognizing future possibilities.

Visual Cues

Visual cues enable us to signal our intentions. By using a certain carpet pattern, we can guide people along a particular path. Likewise, by offering tables and chairs with wheels, we indicate that they could be moved around.

We can shape environments by prompting behavioral norms. This influences the way spaces can be experienced. For example, imagine two reference desks that are exactly the same except that one offers seating for the patron. What message is delivered as a student approaches the librarian? One says, *get comfortable, let's chat.* While with the other, it's, *ask a question, but don't linger.* If the objective is to offer an inviting space, then which of these signifies a more welcoming setting?

The type of chair is another factor—is it a comfortable armchair, or is it an old wobbly barstool? Can the chair be moved adjacent to the librarian (screen-sharing and easy conversation), or is it positioned far away across a big wide desk?

Also consider encoding visual cues by using colors thematically. One example might be using a dramatic color to indicate service points and help kiosks, making it easy for people to instantly know where they can get help. Another idea is using certain colors or patterns on furniture that is movable, communicating to students these items are flexible.

Visual cues aid us in making our spaces more intuitive. All of these small details can have huge implications in terms of how people act and feel within our buildings. And this impacts how well they can accomplish the work they are facing.

The Soul Of A Space

Several years ago I visited a newly renovated library and was surprised that it seemed flat. It was clean and well-organized with modern finishes and furnishings, but something was missing.

That memory stuck with me. After visiting many more libraries and studying retail environments, I recognize today that it lacked ambiance. This intangible quality is so vital. The mood of a space can make or break the experience. In fact, I've visited rundown library buildings filled with people doing exciting things. Their energy was contagious, and the atmosphere compensated for the humble surroundings.

Perhaps the best way to experience ambiance is by going to a mall. Spend an hour browsing in as many clothing stores as you can. Each one presents a different mood and message. Some are energizing while others are subdued. In some you will feel welcomed while in others like an outsider. Consider how crowded they are; how bright or loud. Notice how the clothing is hung, draped, folded, stacked, featured, or otherwise arranged. Is there a conscious attempt at balance? Did you notice any design patterns or visual cues? What was the focal point in each space? Do other people in the store affect the harmony? How is the spatial rhythm different at each location?

All of these factors influence our assumptions and expectations. Does it feel high-end or bargain bin? Is it youthful or sophisticated? Did you feel a sense of belonging? Was there any yearning to make a purchase?

Keep in mind that a store doesn't have to be fancy to inspire high levels of place attachment. For example, a warehouse or discount setting can stimulate excitement: *the thrill of the hunt.* Many people enjoy pawing through racks and boxes to find treasures that others might have missed. Shopping can become like a game that draws you in.

The atmosphere is critical and cannot be overlooked. As we aim to delineate certain intentions and behaviors within our spaces (quiet zones, collaborative hubs, productivity centers, mentoring areas, and so forth) we must consider the different moods associated with these activities. In a sense, we are curating a collection of emotional states throughout our buildings. From retail we learn that in many cases, the atmosphere has more influence on how people feel about merchandise than the actual product itself. We want to be very deliberate with how we design our environments:

Everything matters because it influences the total experience.

AUDIT YOUR ATMOSPHERE

Atmospherics (the effects intended to create a particular mood) are a vital part of our building's program. We should periodically check to ensure that our environment is in tune with our objectives.

Here are a few variables to help you get started. Consider how each element influences the perception of your space and the mood that people are feeling. Also reflect on the changes you can (and can't) make to better align with your purposes.

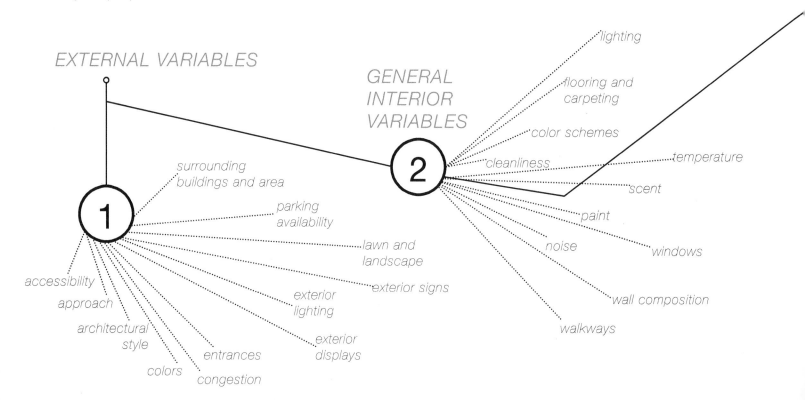

EXTERNAL VARIABLES

GENERAL INTERIOR VARIABLES

1

2

surrounding buildings and area

parking availability

lawn and landscape

exterior signs

accessibility

approach

architectural style

colors

congestion

entrances

exterior lighting

exterior displays

lighting

flooring and carpeting

color schemes

cleanliness

temperature

scent

paint

noise

windows

wall composition

walkways

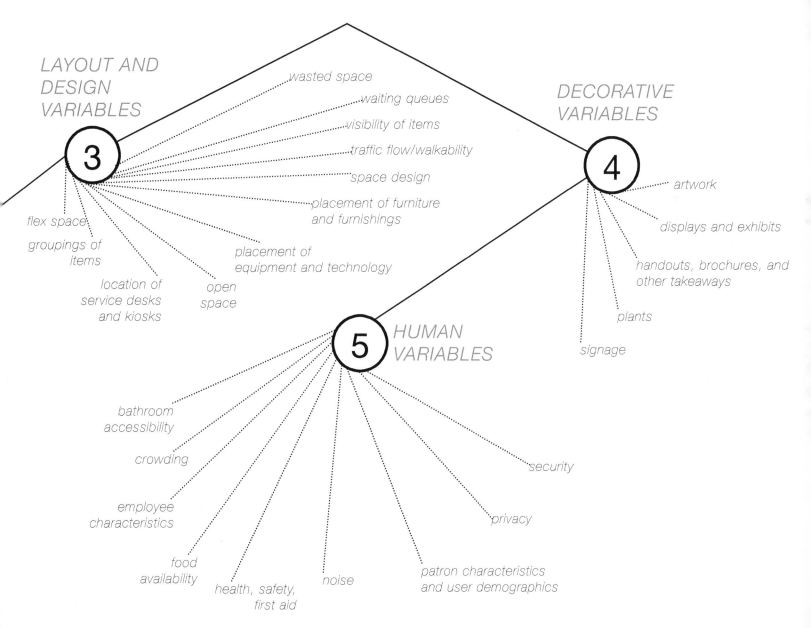

LAYOUT AND DESIGN VARIABLES

3

flex space

groupings of items

location of service desks and kiosks

open space

wasted space

waiting queues

visibility of items

traffic flow/walkability

space design

placement of furniture and furnishings

placement of equipment and technology

DECORATIVE VARIABLES

4

artwork

displays and exhibits

handouts, brochures, and other takeaways

plants

signage

HUMAN VARIABLES

5

bathroom accessibility

crowding

employee characteristics

food availability

health, safety, first aid

noise

patron characteristics and user demographics

privacy

security

45

Can the color of a room make us smarter? One study suggests that it can. Children in classrooms that were painted blue, yellow, green, or orange saw their IQ scores increase, while students in rooms that were white, black, or brown actually saw their scores decrease.

So does color matter?

Color theory is interesting but difficult to interpret and apply. For example, yellow is associated with stress and apprehension, yet it also supposedly stimulates well-being and optimism. But location and culture factor into this too. For example, at Georgia Tech, home of the Yellow Jackets, yellow (gold) holds a significant symbolic representation as one of the school's primary colors. A yellow wall there could engender feelings of pride or belonging, whereas a yellow wall at another university would have a different meaning and provoke a different reaction.

COLOR

Generally speaking, the literature seems to suggest that sensory-rich environments, including vibrant colors, result in greater mental stimulation. So perhaps the particular colors don't matter, but rather the overall harmony within the room. Spaces designed for concentration should probably have a warmer palette than ones seeking to accommodate group conversations. Just as the furniture supporting those purposes would be different, so too should the color spectrum that is deployed.

A Point of View

When Bloomingdale's opened, it was just another department store. In fact, it was actually in the bottom tier for many years. That changed in the 1960s when it developed a new strategy: *become an authoritative store where the merchandise is the central attraction.*

At the time this was a radical step. While its competitors engaged in price wars, Bloomingdale's went high-end. It aspired to shape home and fashion trends by curating unique items and adding a touch of glamour to the shopping experience. Bloomingdale's instantly became a creative force in the industry.

All the best stores have an identity, commonly referred to as a point of view. Essentially it equates to the message or concept they want to convey, from urban chic to rustic country. Is it a specialized boutique or a big box store? Is it sophisticated, playful, edgy, or bargain bin? All of the merchandise, furnishings, and design elements should carry the theme coherently throughout the environment.

As librarians become more invested in commons spaces, we, too, need to consider our message. If we can't focus our point of view into a single clear and conscious phrase, then we can't expect others to interpret it either. Can we be everything to everyone? Retailers would advise that we can't and recommend that we should focus our physical environments on a core user group who share similar interests or intentions.

Larger libraries arguably have an edge in this area because they have the luxury of different floors and zones—a better ability to accommodate hybrid users who can't be pigeonholed or categorized into one core group. In this respect, perhaps the one-size-fits-all commons is a thing of the past, and multiple commons spaces (uncommons spaces?) that blend and flow into each other are the direction forward.

In my library, we've built around the idea that *learning happens here.* We are slowly transforming our main building into an active student-centered environment that accommodates a variety of academic tasks. The space is evolving into a showroom where achievement is highlighted and tools and support are offered to advance assignments and other intellectual or creative pursuits. The act of scholarship is constantly on display wherever you look.

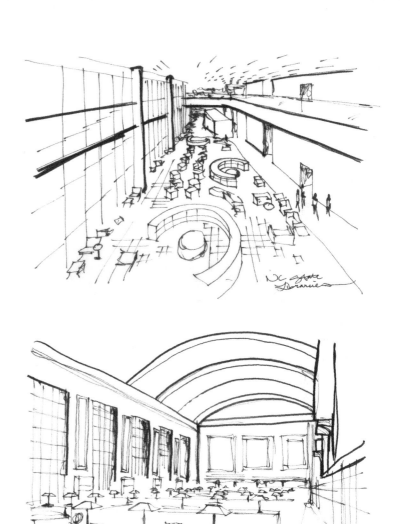

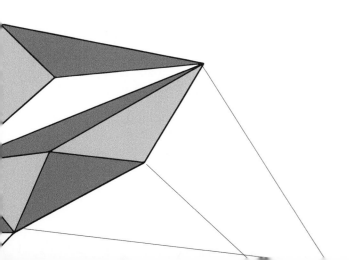

Nurturing The Scholarly Impulse

Impulse purchasing is another intriguing retail phenomenon that we can apply to our learning environments. Simply put, this is the act of making an unplanned purchase. Think of selecting a candy bar while standing in the checkout aisle at your grocery store. What triggers this temptation? People who study shoppers believe that consumers come to stores for *necessities* but leave with *indulgences* that fill previously unrecognized needs. Perhaps grabbing those Reese's Cups is an unconscious signal that you're hungry or that you need something to lift your spirit?

Research suggests that most shoppers make up to 80 percent of their purchase decisions right in the store. Some have only a vague idea of what they want: *I need to get something for dinner tonight.* Others may know the product category they want, but have not yet settled on the specific brand or style: *I need to get some paper towels.* And others make a spur-of-the-moment decision that they must have a specific thing they encounter in passing: *Maybe I need some Oreos.*

The design of the store influences us in a visceral and sensory way. Nearly all unplanned purchases are a result of seeing, touching, hearing, smelling, or tasting something on the premises. In this regard, layouts that encourage browsing and interaction are preferred because they expose consumers to many more possibilities. The deeper and wider the assortment of available products, the more likely we are to make a purchase.

So what does the scholarly impulse look like in the library? Could the arrangement of our furniture entice students to study more? Might we ignite their cultural curiosity with an exhibit? Maybe a display of books or DVDs would result in unplanned borrowing. Seeing a classmate could spur on a brainstorming session. Seeing a professor could result in informal mentoring. Observing new wearable technology could spark interest. Watching someone move a portable whiteboard could incite a similar behavior. A peer assistant roving the floor could result in asking for help. We've even encountered students enrolling in a particular course based on library exhibits that featured tools and content from the class.

Think of this as filling our spaces with small invitations that trigger intellectual, creative, or cultural curiosity. Surrounding our students and others with these happenstances extends the value and mystique of the library as a serendipitous environment where chance encounters gratify the mind.

Is It What You Thought It Would Be?

Meeting user expectations can be challenging. Not just their functional needs, but those on a deeper, more symbolic level. When the familiar (historical) role of a library clashes with its evolving identity, confusion or disappointment can emerge. Not only are we changing physical spaces, we're also challenging preconceptions of what a library is supposed to be.

Retailers might suggest that we have an issue with congruence. The popular notion of libraries as quiet spaces filled with books doesn't match the commons model that has emerged. People carry certain expectations, and as they move through our buildings, they are constantly evaluating the library against their assumptions. The problem occurs when someone is expecting to find a particular experience but encounters something completely different.

This concept of congruence transcends mere user satisfaction. Research suggests that the way people feel within a space has a direct impact on their emotional and cognitive states. The more in sync they are with their surroundings, the better they can utilize them for productive behavior. We interpret and give meaning to the environments we encounter. In this manner, differences among individuals and groups lie not in how they behave but in how they perceive the library.

I think Institutional culture is a major factor. For instance, at certain schools, a grand reading room is probably ideal, while on other campuses a technology-oriented environment is more desirable. Curriculum matters too. If the majority of students are focused on reading and writing, then quiet individual spaces are likely in high demand. Yet if assignments are more collaborative or require a wide range of software tools, then obviously a different setting is needed.

The better we are able to articulate our intentions (our point of view), the easier it is for students and faculty to understand how libraries are changing. Since we need to accommodate many different needs, retailers would advise us to either designate districts (the quiet floor, the noisy floor, the technology floor, etc.) or to develop a neutral environment allowing for versatile use by the maximum number of people.

Conflict arises through misunderstandings of the intended use of specific spaces. Additionally the same stimulus can produce widely different perspectives. Multifunctional space can be ideal for accommodating diverse needs, but it can also create disagreement if intentions are unclear.

At Virginia Tech we face a challenge of students expecting more enclosed group study rooms, yet due to our facilities infrastructure (HVAC) we are unable to accommodate more demand. Our solution has been to offer over five hundred tables of various shapes and sizes. Students can mix and match with portable whiteboards, privacy screens, and monitors to create unique group settings. This aligns with our point of view that people should personalize the environment for the particular learning task at hand. In this manner we are encouraging students to shape the space however they need it for whatever they are trying to do.

Primed For Success

Can we set people up to succeed? Maybe.

Priming is a tactic that advertisers use to instill desire. It is the process of exposing people to ideas (or values) with the goal of influencing their beliefs and behaviors. Retailers employ these tactics by attempting to prime people to feel happy, hungry, or generous while in their stores. Obviously they want to encourage sales, but could this approach be used for other intentions?

Studies suggest that simply asking people about their behaviors can influence them. For example, inquiring about consumption of fatty foods reduces their short-term intake or asking people how often they floss increases dental hygiene for a few days.

So could we prime people to feel reflective or creative? What if upon entering the library students felt inspired or confident? Could a visit to our facilities be associated with the notion of accomplishment?

Picture this: You enter the lobby and are greeted with a digital art installation created as part of an independent study. A little further in, a group is hosting a poster session review and talking about their bioethics research. Around the corner a student is demonstrating a video game she developed as part of her senior capstone. Down the hall a student organization is holding a panel discussion on gender equality. As you glance around, you notice that the walls are covered with a variety of projects from many different disciplines: art, science, history, engineering, and business. Now imagine studying in this environment where peer achievements are showcased and celebrated. You are a part of all this.

As we think about next-generation learning environments, it is critical that we give this idea of priming some thought. I see our guiding objective as creating the conditions that give users the opportunity to find success.

While we want to present our facilities as great places to study and get work done—those activities can happen elsewhere too. Instead, the library can be framed as an intellectual transistor, an environment filled with learning energy, which you can plug in to. By becoming a part of it, you in turn help to perpetuate that spirit of the place. In short, by being there and being productively engaged, you help prime the location for others sharing the experience. They in turn inspire you to be more productive as well.

Visit any major department store, and you will likely observe vendor shops (typically for cosmetics, apparel, accessories, or electronics) that stand out from the rest of the environment. These mini boutiques or "stores within a store" are designed to reflect a particular brand. Sephora, Chanel, Estée Lauder, MAC, and Dior are a few popular examples.

Research (and profits) confirm that these locations are successful ventures. They attract customers who otherwise would not visit the department store, creating an opportunity to cross sell or showcase other merchandise. The shops also bring elements of prestige and exclusivity, heightening the mood and atmosphere. The top brands benefit by having direct contact with new customers.

It is interesting to consider how libraries are applying the store-within-a-store model. Like department stores, our buildings attract a wide audience and serve as an ideal platform for adjacent partnerships. External units, such as writing centers, multimedia labs, and IT help desks, are quite common.

Other branded environments, such as makerspaces, digital humanities centers, visualization labs, and data studios, are emerging as well.

As our physical footprint continues to open, the store-within-a-store model presents some intriguing possibilities. I can imagine library buildings hosting an assortment of shops such as flexible classrooms, specialized labs, and consultation services in conjunction with particular disciplines or academic partners.

Libraries can also host outposts from partners such as faculty development offices, instruction design studios, assessment services, grant support, undergraduate research, tutoring, and so on. The library collection in this scenario brings together a variety of tools, resources, and expertise necessary to advance teaching, learning, research, and service. People who do not typically visit the library may encounter some appeal. And likewise, regular library users may find some new service offerings that then enhance their productivity.

a-store

Away From The Desk

Roving service isn't new, but it is interesting to see how retailers are deploying it. Many large stores are encouraging their staff to move out from behind service counters and engage people directly on the sales floor. Equipped with tablet computers, employees are empowered to make on-the-spot sales or can instantly order specialized items for customers. Through this approach, sales staff can move seamlessly throughout the entire shopping journey—from browsing and discovery, to selection and purchasing.

Librarians are thinking along these lines too and considering a more expanded role. We want to become more embedded across learning, teaching, and research practices happening on our campuses.

As we consider our physical environments, a team of student assistants could work similarly, roaming the library looking for people to help. With a mobile device in tow, they could collect statistics, photos, interviews, and other data to support improvement efforts. They could set up for events, clean up small spills, and adjust furniture arrangements accordingly. The student team might also provide basic technology support—wireless access, printing, and scanning. And they could retrieve books, give tours, provide directions, and offer other types of assistance.

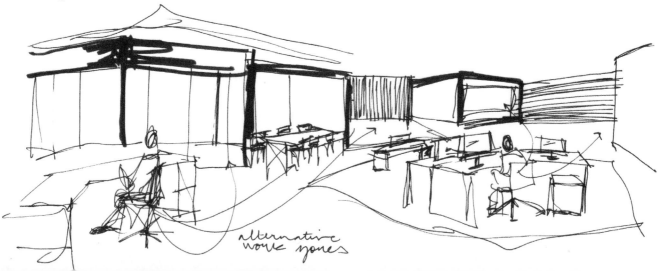

alternative work zones

Perhaps some of these students are hired for specific skills, such as fluency with statistical packages or certain academic backgrounds. In this manner, student peer leaders transcend being our eyes and ears and are empowered with a degree of autonomy that could spark some new directions. With guidance they could evolve from *students helping students* into a group that is focused on the well-being of library users. Through developing a sense of ownership, they would strive to improve the overall experience. Working with library commons managers, they would enhance the learning atmosphere by interpreting the emergent needs of the community and addressing them in real time. This form of action-minded service allows the library to be more nimble, proactive, and engaging.

Omni Channel

For years, retailers have tried to recreate the in-store shopping experience online, but now that is changing. Today, progressive stores are transforming from places that stock and sell merchandise into digitally integrated environments designed to engage and entertain. As buying items online becomes easier, physical stores are being reinvented.

One of the major disruptions has been how we decide what to purchase. In the past, shopping operated like a funnel; people were exposed to a limited number of items and they weighed their options based on what was available on a shelf. Today the path resembles a pinball where plugged-in shoppers bounce around between many different touch points, gathering scraps of information from online reviews, social media, and other content that shapes their decision making.

Stores are adopting an omni channel approach. This strategy is the attempt at a seamless melding of the sensory benefits of physical stores with the information-rich experience of online shopping. It aims to offer a continuous flow across brands, formats, and devices. Visiting a store and its website should share a great degree of consistency in the look, layout, language, policies, and services. Being able to purchase something online and return it to the store (or vice versa) is becoming common practice. This helps build customer loyalty as well as operational efficiencies.

The eyewear company Warby Parker provides an intriguing omni channel case study. It sells glasses online, but during specific times of the year hosts pop-up shops. At these locations visitors can receive eye exams and style suggestions from store associates. Yet there is no inventory onsite. All payments are collected and orders are processed using the same website available to everyone everywhere. Glasses are typically mailed within a week.

In this manner, the physical space serves as a showroom for an online product. The retail operation occurs on the regular website, but the temporary physical location enables new customers to be introduced to the eyewear (and the Web presence) while also allowing current customers to come in and deepen their relationship.

This theme resonates within academic libraries too. Increasingly, more of our collection offerings are shifting to digital platforms as well as off-campus warehouses. Our future and present challenge is developing physical environments that represent these diverse holdings. Furthermore, we can't think of databases, digital libraries, and other web content as separate; it's all a unified experience in the eyes of our users. A committed integrated approach to breaking down traditional silos will inspire us to design new service layers, attitudes, and practices for more seamless interactions.

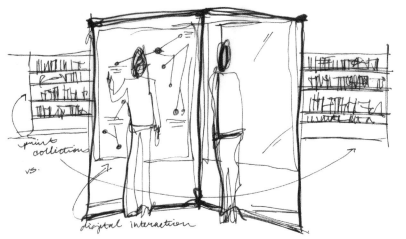

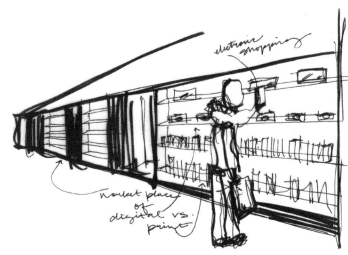

are libraries becoming storefronts for digital collections?

Curating

Are your public spaces successful? How do you know? This is the question we're all trying to answer. And quite honestly, it's probably the most important question for us to explore. Not only does it lead to improving our daily operations, but it also allows us to address the value that libraries create.

Right now we can point to gate counts, log-ins, and service transactions. We can show photographs of packed study areas and upload video testimonials of students and faculty praising our facilities. Survey results might even suggest that users are highly satisfied. But does any of this prove that we are successful?

Retailers are facing similar questions. While they have an enormous toolkit of metrics at their disposal, they lack clear methods for understanding the customer experience. Data-driven approaches are insufficient for addressing the nonlinear and seemingly spontaneous nature of purchase-making decisions. They also engage in ethnographic studies (similar to those conducted by libraries) as an attempt to better understand how people think and act in their spaces. Still, questions remain about the effectiveness of their physical environments on enhancing shopping.

Assessment is tricky and can be highly subjective— not to mention it's problematic to treat users as a homogenous group: Needs and wants can shift hour by hour or even overlap. Individuals can be several different types of users within a single visit. This makes it challenging to articulate the success of our environments.

I think we need to shift attention away from *the performance of our spaces* and instead concentrate on *the performance of the people using our spaces.* If we apply a retail lens, our buildings become a loose framework of differentiated zones, each with clear intentions. Just as a department store features home goods, apparel, or cosmetics, we might focus on actions such as brainstorming, group projects, or composition. Even relaxation, reflection, and stress

Behaviors

relief are valid concerns of the academic experience with an increasing concern for student mental health and well-being. Consider the range of activities that you want to emphasize and then shape (and encode) these themes into your design.

Defining activity groupings unlocks a new path for inquiry. Now we can explore different questions centered on a set of outcomes. For example, what factors stimulate brainstorming? Or, how can we help groups work together more effectively? And, what are the different assignments where students need to compose (essays, graphics, data, code, video, audio), and how does the environment propel them? Our focus here becomes pursuing deeper insights into people's work cycles and then creating optimal settings.

We should think of our role as curating behaviors and then measure against those objectives. This emphasis on intentionality enables us to pinpoint how our spaces and services have a direct impact on the wider enterprise.

The only way we can measure the success of our space is through the capabilities it creates.

Anticipate needs-don't just meet them.

The goal of assessment should be to find more questions, not just answers.

Personalization

Retailers feel that in order to be competitive they need to develop long-lasting relationships with their customers, generating repeat business. There is an emerging interest in mass personalization, which aspires to create unique experiences for shoppers. The industry is experimenting with tools and techniques allowing it to determine customer needs and preferences in order to offer enhanced services.

The rise of online shopping and the accessibility of big data have ushered in this new era. Today, physical spaces desire to be like web spaces in which visitors carry in profiles that volunteer personal information and shopping histories. All this can be applied to heighten the experience. Ideally the store knows you have entered and you automatically receive customized recommendations and other attention. Conceptually, the music, lighting, and other atmospheric elements change based on who is in the store.

Retailers are also digging into the data. Target, for example, can predict major life events (pregnancy, marriage, new home, new job) based on purchase patterns. Whenever we experience these periods of great change, our buying habits change too. Retailers are using these insights to influence us and encourage us to establish new habits. This makes me think of the major changes in our community (first semester at college, transferring in, starting graduate school, or beginning the tenure-track process) and how libraries can customize offerings for these known life events.

Obviously, privacy concerns are especially pertinent to us. We value confidentiality and want people to feel safe in our spaces. And yet, we also have a desire to connect, to make the library relevant on an individual level. The better we understand the people using our buildings, the better positioned we are to provide them with relevant collections and services.

I explored this theme with a student advisory group, and they downplayed privacy concerns. They have to swipe their IDs to access residential spaces, dining halls, gyms, labs, and certain classrooms. It seemed logical to them to do the same in the library. In fact, they wanted data to be useful for them in terms of a dashboard that indicates how busy the library currently is and the availability of laptops, study rooms, seating, and other services.

One student shared that if she was in a bad mood or felt stressed out, she would welcome the library attempting to cheer her up: an infrastructure where the atmospherics adjusted based on mood and behaviors. Perhaps that is taking personalization too far, but at some point this technology could become ubiquitous. There is a line of manipulation that we don't want to cross, but it is an interesting concept to ponder: a smart building that can adapt itself based on the circumstances and activities happening within it. Or perhaps libraries become the counter-trend—one of the few places where individuality and autonomy are respected and honored, and where people can remain anonymous.

Responsive Space

We often think of responsive design in terms of web development. This is the act of crafting web content to change based upon the device from which it is viewed. A webpage seen on a laptop looks different when seen on a smartphone. The architecture and user experience transforms based on the technological circumstances.

Can we apply this concept to our physical spaces as well? What if our environments could adapt based upon the time of the day or the point in the semester? In the morning, many academic libraries are filled with individuals prepping for class, whereas later in the

day groups form to work on assignments together. Likewise, the spatial demands that users have during the initial weeks of a semester are very different from those during the final weeks. What if our commons areas could be constantly reconfigured to accommodate these evolving needs?

Mall merchants apply this concept by regularly changing their front-of-store displays. A bookstore alternates between titles on health, travel, finances, parenting, sports, technology, music, and popular culture in hopes of attracting different customer segments frequenting at different times of the day. I've witnessed this same tactic used by shoe and apparel shops as well.

We can also respond to seasonal needs that emerge throughout the year. A library could host tutors or therapy dogs before big exams or résumé reviewers before a career fair. Pop-up support related to academic advising, registration, orientation, financial aid, study abroad, or e-portfolios could be hosted around critical deadlines. Consider how you might harness the temporal properties of your spaces and how the same space can serve different needs at different times.

This approach presents some interesting concepts for us to consider. If we interpret our mission as connecting people with information, then the notion of responsive design is part of a natural evolution. We are not only providing appropriate workspace and suitable collections, but also addressing information gaps about campus-wide services and raising awareness of available options.

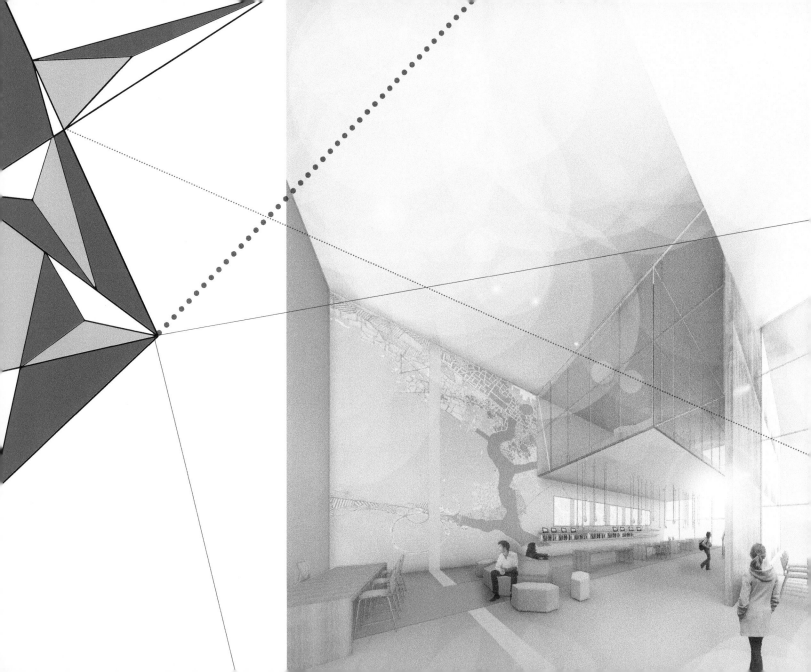

DESIGN
CONCEPTS

Examining libraries through different lenses is a way to stimulate creativity. It releases any personal attachments and preconceptions that we have and allows us to think more openly. This is advantageous when we want to be strategic and contemplate disruptive circumstances.

Spending time exploring different scenarios better prepares us for unexpected twists and turns that the future unveils. By allowing ourselves to wander off the beaten path, we just might stumble upon opportunities wanting to be discovered.

These concepts are meant to serve as a jumping-off point. They are presented with some ambiguity so you and your team can reflect on which elements make sense for your communities. Here is a simplified way that I use to describe their differences.

Let's take an emerging technology like virtual reality headgear (such as Oculus Rift and Microsoft's HoloLens) and compare the interactions in each space.

KNOWLEDGE SHOWROOMS

KNOWLEDGE STUDIOS

KNOWLEDGE BOUTIQUES

KNOWLEDGE SALONS

Libraries can be a blend of all of these different modes, but to initiate brainstorming it is helpful to look at the various interconnected thematic concepts as separate extremes.

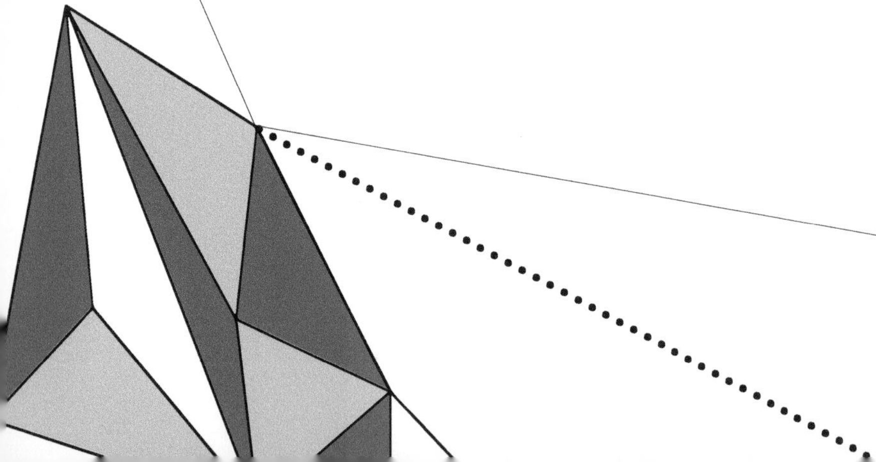

SHOWROOMS

In the showroom setting, you can test out the equipment, see a demo, and perhaps borrow equipment for a few weeks.

STUDIOS

In the studio environment, you could work with classmates to develop code and test it out.

BOUTIQUES

In the boutique, a technologist would work with you directly to design your project.

SALONS

In the salon, you would attend a lecture about artificial realities and experience an immersive exhibit.

KNOWLEDGE
SHOWROOMS

Knowledge Showrooms are stimulating environments designed to celebrate intellectual and creative endeavors. The key attribute is their inviting and inspiring atmosphere. These spaces are filled with scholarly works in many formats and across all disciplines. While final outputs are highlighted, emphasis is also given to processes—how the work is done.

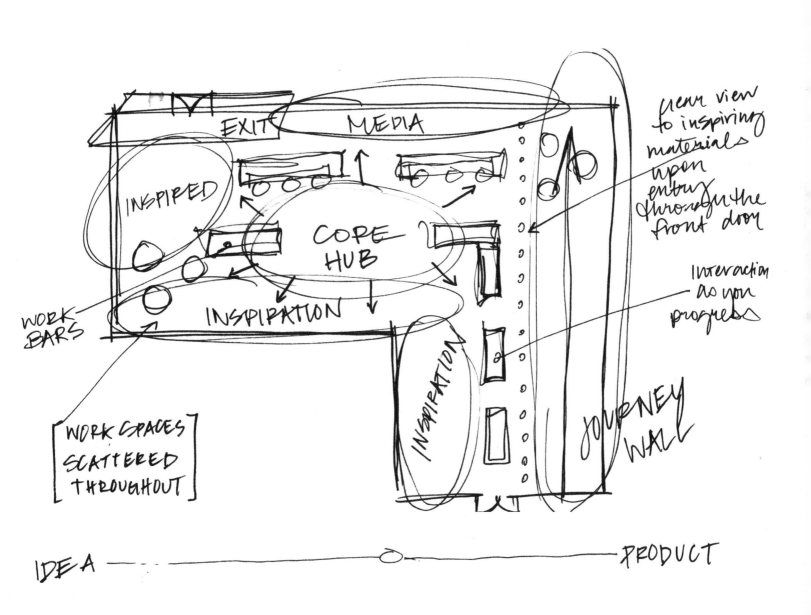

EXIT   MEDIA

INSPIRED

CORE HUB

INSPIRATION

WORK BARS

INSPIRATION

WORK SPACES
SCATTERED
THROUGHOUT

clear view
to inspiring
materials
upon
entry
through the
front door

Interaction
as you
progress

JOURNEY WALL

IDEA ——————————————o—————————————— PRODUCT

While there are some museum-like qualities inherent in this concept, the environment is meant to be interactive, in effect, like a World's Fair. It aspires to make scholarship tangible and reusable. For example, not only can you view a visualization installation, but you can also remix the data for your own project. You can also contribute your own content for others to explore and utilize.

This variation presents a wide spectrum of tools and resources for people to discover. Emerging technologies are available to test out. The latest furniture constantly cycles in. New knowledge formats are featured for experimentation. The aim is to offer an intellectually rich environment that piques curiosity and entices visitors to make new connections.

Intermingled with the various displays and artifacts are a variety of commons areas. Clusters of productivity spaces are sprinkled throughout the floors, resulting in an atmosphere that is incredibly motivating. Not only are you surrounded by great achievements, but also you can see how your own efforts become a part of the ever-expanding lineage of knowledge.

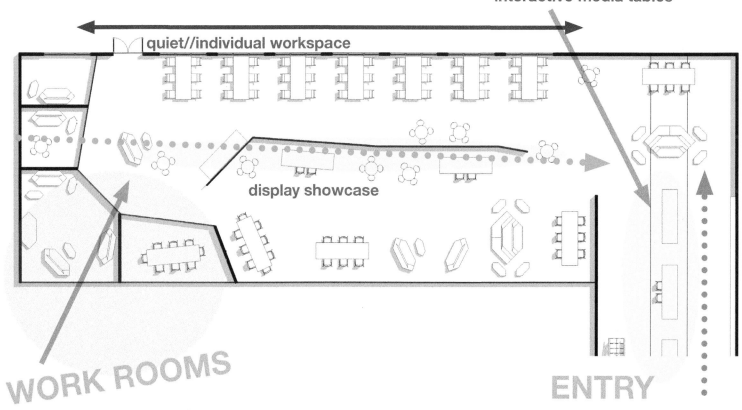

interactive media tables

quiet//individual workspace

display showcase

WORK ROOMS

ENTRY

KNOWLEDGE
STUDIOS

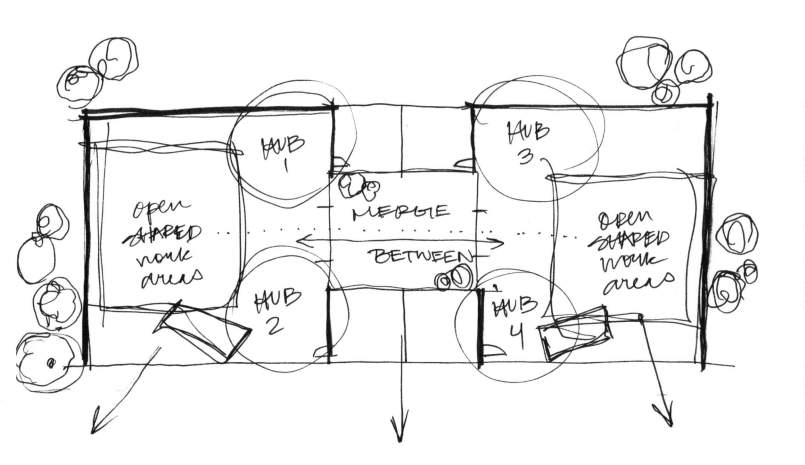

open ~~shared~~ work areas

HUB 1

HUB 2

MERGE

BETWEEN

HUB 3

HUB 4

open ~~shared~~ work areas

Knowledge studios are a collection of offices, labs, and service centers bringing together diverse projects from across the campus. In this variation, libraries become an intellectual infrastructure providing space and support to advance science, scholarship, and creative outputs.

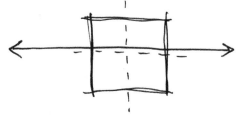

Disciplines come together through [SHARED SPACE].

+ Brainstorming Space
+ Collaboration Space

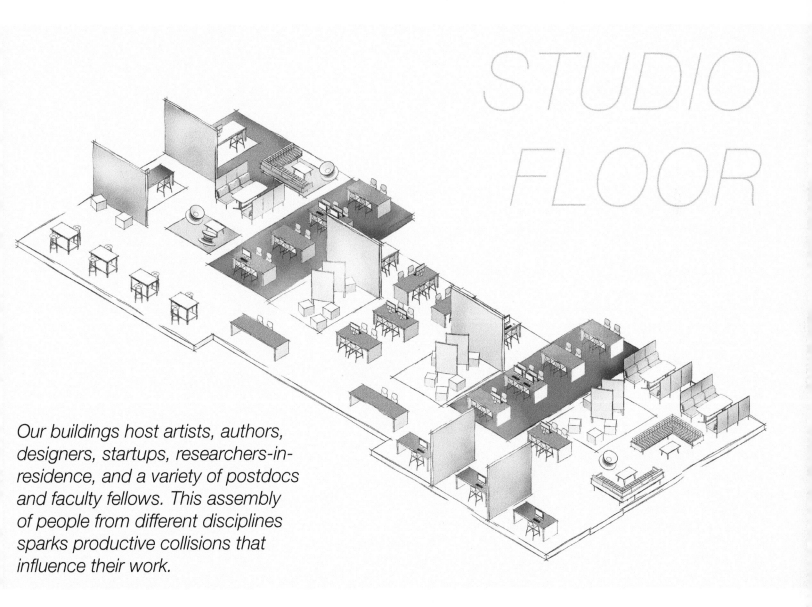

Our buildings host artists, authors, designers, startups, researchers-in-residence, and a variety of postdocs and faculty fellows. This assembly of people from different disciplines sparks productive collisions that influence their work.

While the facility retains some print collections and commons areas, a predominant amount of space is dedicated to project-based work such as undergraduate research, service learning, and capstone courses. Lounges and labs support broad academic disciplines: engineering, science, arts and humanities, social sciences. There are also crossover opportunities, such as agriculture students working with biology students on a public health paper, or linguists working with MBA and political science students to measure how election rhetoric impacts the stock market.

The knowledge studio becomes a place to mix and remix ideas, collections, skills, and perspectives.

Librarians play an active role in shaping the experience and partnering in the work being done. They are deeply involved with integrating tools, resources, and spaces that propel learning and research, assessing the progress in real time.

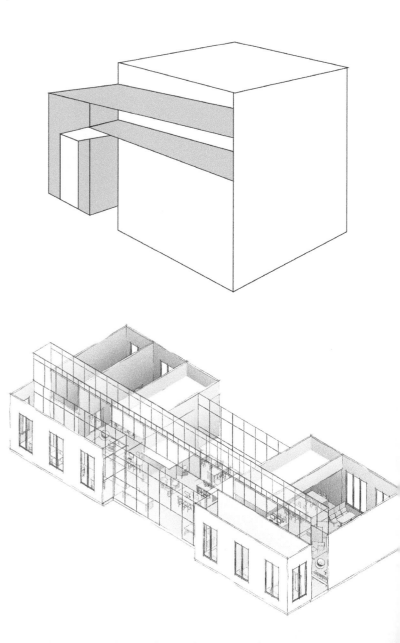

multitude of services interacting with one another.

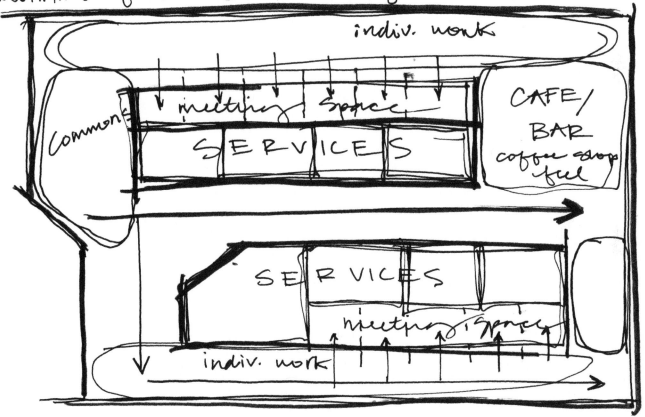

indiv. work

Commons

meeting Space

S E R V I C E S

CAFE/
BAR
coffee shop
feel

S E R V I C E S

meeting Space

indiv. work

Knowledge Boutiques offer specialized services tailored to specific audiences. The intention is to provide unique environments combined with personalized assistance. This scenario recognizes that library buildings often cannot accommodate their entire community and, therefore, evolve to focus on particular functions.

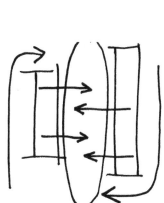

service centric space
meeting / common zones for people to
come together

Boutique labs can support faculty in many ways. Technologists and project managers converge to help researchers implement new directions. Data consultants and designers assist them in visualizing their work. Grant writers, publishing experts, and public relations professionals aid in sponsored research applications. Instructional designers and web application developers support them in establishing new pedagogical practices and incorporating new literacies in their courses.

In this manner, libraries become full-service centers that aid research, teaching, and creative projects. The objective is to support faculty along the entire journey—from concept through implementation and beyond. This places greater emphasis on librarians as partners across faculty processes and practices.

On the student side, the boutique offers a marketplace of support services such as a writing center, a multimedia design lab, an IT help desk, a presentation lab, academic tutoring, a GIS center, a data visualization lab, and other specialized agencies. Librarians are entwined with learning and productivity. The emphasis is geared toward building interrelated and transferrable skills.

KNOWLEDGE BOUTIQUES

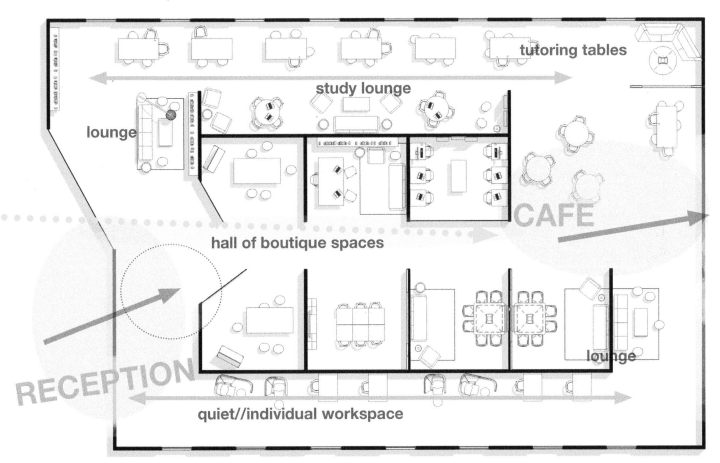

tutoring tables

study lounge

lounge

hall of boutique spaces

CAFE

RECEPTION

lounge

quiet//individual workspace

KNOWLEDGE
SALONS

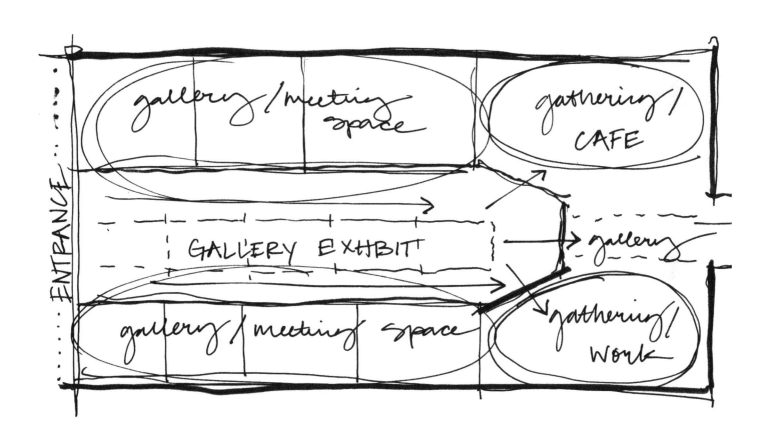

ENTRANCE

gallery / meeting space

gathering / CAFE

GALLERY EXHIBIT

gallery

gallery / meeting space

gathering / Work

89

Knowledge Salons are hubs for intellectual gatherings and spaces that spark curiosity. The objective is to bring people together to share and explore questions and, thus, push the boundaries of knowledge. The social element is critical with the aspiration to assemble people with diverse backgrounds and skill sets to mix and mingle, resulting in generative thinking and stimulating new ideas and projects.

This concept blends together the conversational nature of the eighteenth-century French salons with the golden age of department stores. As these new shopping experiences emerged, they served as indoor parks. Upscale stores featured galleries with works by Pablo Picasso, Georges Braque, and Maurice Utrillo. They hosted musical performances, lectures, and tearooms. Today, flagship stores like Prada and Burberry present their retail environments as entertainment spaces where music recitals, theatrical performances, and fashion shows can be experienced. Even hardware stores like Home Depot and Lowe's host events for people to talk about their projects and get advice.

The objective is to foster community. The library becomes more like a cultural center, not just because of its collections, but also through the act of connecting people and encouraging the social-intellectual exchange. We nurture the companionship of curious people through panel discussions, exhibits and installations, films, debates, and other forms of interaction.

MAKER SPACE

Beyond conversations, the Knowledge Salon also provides space for demonstrations, experimentation, workshops, symposia, and hands-on learning. Students and faculty can share their current projects and solicit advice (and partnerships) for future endeavors.

The critical concept is that providing spaces, collections, and services is not enough. Librarians serve as hosts and programmatic partners weaving together the intellectual fabric of our campus community. We embrace an active role in shaping the program, stimulating the activities, and guiding productive outcomes.

interdisciplinary fusion

ENCODING
ENVIRONM

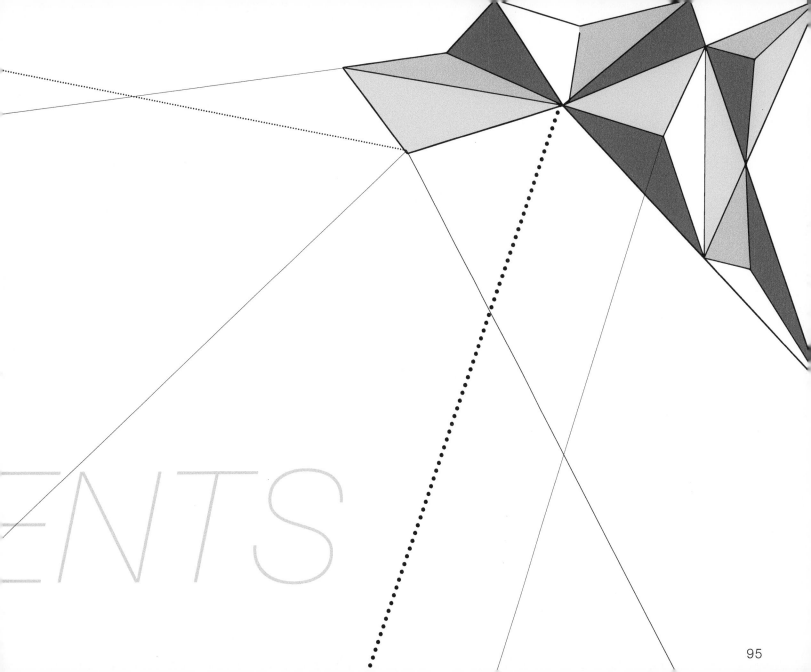

ENTS

When we decode, we take something that is unintelligible and make it coherent. From disorder we form context.

I find this idea of transference fascinating. Now let's reverse it. Can we encode something? Let's take something tangible, like a large open room, and infuse it with a message. Fill a vacant space (like a blank canvas) with a sense of significance.

I'm interested in outfitting a structure that embodies a large palette of emotions. This is a tough challenge: taking physical spaces and transforming them beyond their functional purpose. But when we study this through the eyes of the retailer, interior designer, or urban planner, we know it is possible.

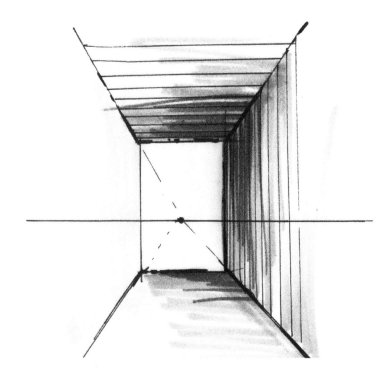

So how might we program libraries in this regard? What are the sentiments and significance that we aspire to nurture?

When planning a new building, addition, or other project, I recommend investing ample time in considering the emotions you want to cultivate—and not just the furniture, finishes, and equipment. We have an opportunity to do more than design and program environments: We can encode them too.

Here are a few attributes to get you thinking.

FLOURISH

A trip to the library is an intellectual pilgrimage. It is a commitment to getting something accomplished. This environment transports you into a higher mental state, allowing you to tap into greater focus. This atmosphere boosts productivity and self-confidence.

INTROSPECTION

The library can counterbalance the always-on digital lifestyle. The space offers an increasingly rare opportunity for people to be alone, to unplug, to reflect and examine thoughts, feelings, or ideas. There is a beauty and comfort in this quietness. This might be one of the few places on campus where you can pause and appreciate being by yourself.

RESTORATION

This environment focuses on mental renewal. It offers a place to decompress, rejuvenate, and heal the spirit. Consider it an invitation into tranquility, the opportunity to reduce stress and personal burdens. The library provides you with a chance to refill your sense of hope and empowers you to face the world with a greater amount of calm. Restoration can also be re-energizing—reaffirming your sense of purpose or finding a new one.

FLOW

You come to this environment for deep concentration. You are absorbed and actively making progress on assignments. Challenging tasks are faced, and the effort delivers a sense of exhilaration. You are in the zone.

WONDER

This environment stimulates curiosity and encourages serendipitous encounters, while simultaneously elevating aspirations. You discover the unimagined, unlocking new possibilities. You are surrounded by a sense of awe, and a mental tug leaves you wanting to know more.

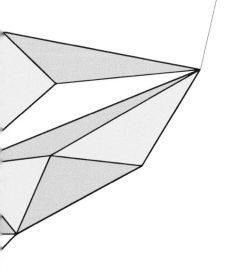

INCLUSIVITY

The library building presents a sense of openness: Everyone can use it. Regardless of your academic major, departmental affiliation, demographics, residential accommodations, or personal beliefs, all are welcome here. The space encourages different perspectives to collide by hosting a diverse mix of people involved in varied activities.

PROVOCATION

This library isn't passive; it is an active instrument seeking to provoke. In this space you are challenged and confronted with new frames of reference. Your values are tested. Critical thinking is manifested here. The library propels people into service, activism, and civic engagement.

ALTRUISM

Imagine an environment where people go out of their way to help others. A tone is set to encourage supportive behaviors; positive language and visual elements are encoded across the landscape. A gracious spirit surrounds library residents; they reciprocate the generosity that they witness (paying it forward) in this setting filled with kindness.

BELONGING

This environment fosters a culture of togetherness. You feel validated by seeing others engaged in similar work. This social proof reinforces positive effort, celebrates achievement, and invites all to participate. You feel connected and part of the community.

EMPOWERMENT

CONVERGENCE

Here you find a rich ecosystem filled with diverse collections, people, and tools placed together in a shared setting. The adjacency of these different domains nurtures your creative spirit and sparks inspiration. The close clustering of resources ushers the free flow of information resulting in random and unpredictable interactions that cannot happen anywhere else on campus.

ADAPTATION

The environment becomes what you need. It is a giant sandbox that encourages continuous shape-shifting. The library is a living prototype. The space is intended to be reconfigurable, and it adapts to a multitude of diverse tasks throughout the day. The implicit permission to make changes is encoded into the space. It won't work as intended if the design is imposing, forbidding, or rigid.

AGENCY

This setting offers you a sense of control and ownership. Once you determine what you need, you can alter the situation. The space teaches that you can influence your environment—mold it to become more accommodating for the task at hand. You realize that you possess influence—the ability to change the world around you. It is the embodiment of a democratic atmosphere.

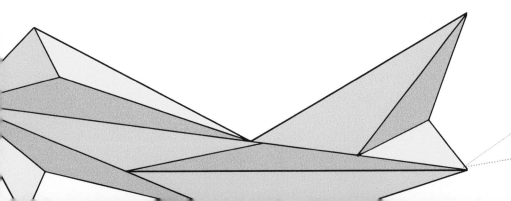

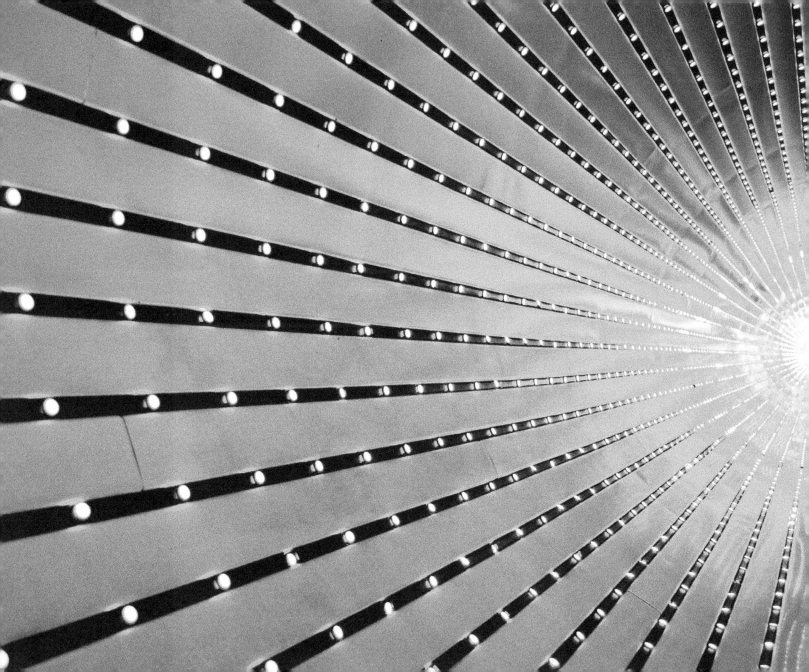

BUT CAN WE ENCODE?

The more I've studied architecture and environmental psychology, the more conscious I've become about the spaces I inhabit. Sometimes my feelings about a room are very obvious and instantly apparent. *I hate it. I love it.*

Yet in other instances my emotion ebbs and flows with continued use. For instance, there is an experimental classroom on my campus that I initially favored. But once the designer of that space moved on to another university, the context of the room changed, and now I find it a challenging place to visit. Even though the furniture is the same, my experience is completely different.

Some spaces grow on us. And sometimes we grow out of certain spaces. But the overarching idea I've gathered is that the users (residents or visitors) of a space are the only ones who can attribute its meaning.

Individuals interpret and define an environment, and this constitutes a moving target. Meaning is attributed in a person's perceptions largely based on what she carries with her into the space, not just her sensory experience in the moment. It is represented in the relationships developed while working across the landscape. And these relationships evolve over time. In this way, it's the experiences lived in it that creates significance.

Perhaps the best we can do is set a tone and invite people in. We can craft perceptual cues and offer some context, but ultimately what a space becomes and how people feel about it is out of our hands. Only the users of the library building can truly encode it with meaning. Our role is to give them the tools and freedom to do so. And to remain attuned to the usage and vibe of the environments to ensure they continue to be effective.

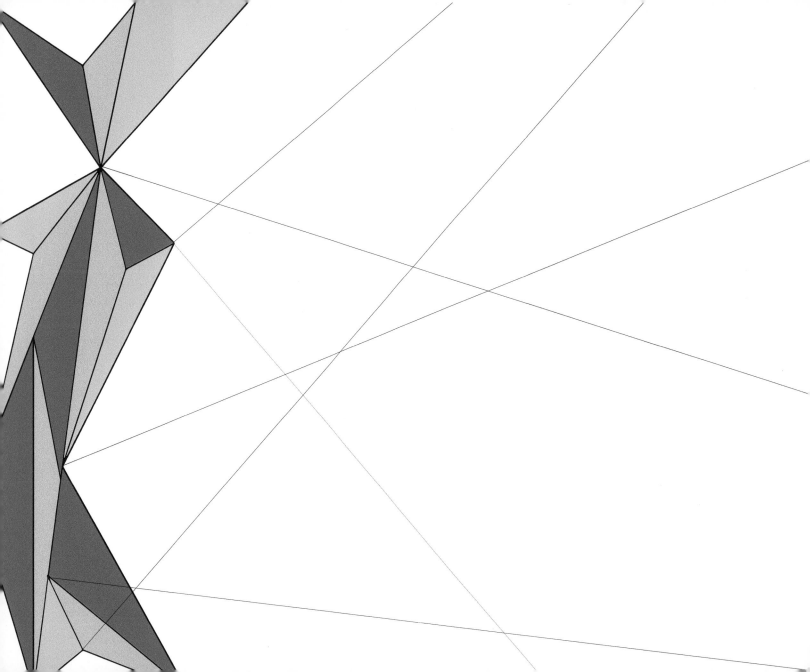

CONCEPTUAL
TRANSITIONS

The migration of scholarly content to digital domains has ushered in many dramatic changes across libraries. While we have witnessed many advances since the emergence of the Web, I can imagine a handful of additional transitions on our horizon.

This section serves as a conversation starter for what lies ahead.

From Third Place to Magnet Place

Many library learning space managers have adopted the third place metaphor when describing their buildings. These social-oriented environments are in between home (first place) and work (second place) where people come to connect and unwind. Third place establishments typically include bars, barbershops, coffee shops, and parks.

While certain aspects of the third place narrative (welcoming, free or inexpensive, conversation-friendly, and open to all) are applicable to our buildings, I've always struggled with this label. In my experience talking with and observing library users, they are almost always there to do something related to work: papers, projects, readings, problem sets, and so forth. Certainly some recreational activities occur, but largely, I think that students and faculty view their library as connected with their academic pursuits: an extension of their labs and classrooms.

Furthermore, the third place label does not communicate a sense of importance, especially when competing for limited institutional funding. It has always sounded to me as if it were low priority and discretionary.

Perhaps magnet place is a more suitable metaphor? These are gathering spots where people with shared interests, pursuits, or cultural yearnings come together. We flock to these environments knowing that we can learn from others as well as demonstrate and apply our own knowledge and skills. These locations exude magnetic-like properties, attracting individuals with similar outlooks or dispositions. We congregate in these places specifically because of the people who inhabit them. It satisfies in us a sense of belonging.

Another interesting layer to this concept comes from neuroscience, which suggests that the people around us affect how we feel and how we act. When we are around others, we are plugged into a neural Wi-Fi, a feedback loop that has an impact on our thoughts and collective behaviors.

Scientists observing people in public areas detected physical synchronies (gestures, expressions) forming shared rhythm of movements. Our minds are mental sponges soaking up the moods and activities of those surrounding us. We mirror what we see. For instance, seeing others at the gym pushes us to run harder or lift more. Being around other shoppers encourages us to make more purchases. Research suggests that we subconsciously imagine ourselves acting out whatever we see happening around us.

Reconceiving libraries as magnet spaces where people plug into a neural Wi-Fi presents us with some interesting opportunities. If we are around studious people, then we will feel more inclined toward that mind-set as well. Likewise, if you are around people who are brainstorming or doing creative work, then that will affect you too. Just witnessing someone reading a book or writing on a whiteboard causes us to visualize ourselves doing that same action.

People are becoming increasingly attracted to libraries because of what they can do inside of them. As we aim to encode our commons areas, this encourages us to be more conscious of both the emotional and functional landscapes that we are creating.

After considering the behaviors and outcomes that we want to encourage, we optimize our environments for those activities.

The more explicit we can be about our intentions, the better our community can understand and utilize them. Model the behaviors that you want to see.

From Commons To Community

While libraries have traditionally included reading rooms, group study rooms, and quiet carrels, over the last two decades we have witnessed an explosion of commons spaces. With the introduction of cafés, computers, comfortable seating, and flexible furniture, as well as multimedia labs, IT help, tutors, and writing centers, the topography of library environments has changed dramatically. We are becoming the living room of campus where students gather, hang out, and study together.

While this movement has generated a lot of excitement, my concern is that we are focusing too much on *the commons* and not enough on the people using *the commons*. When I talk with librarians about their facilities, they often mention the technology, furnishings, and partnerships. Of course these items and relationships are necessary, but generally the conversations center on the "stuff in the space" and not the moods and behaviors that we are trying to curate. The focus is on features rather than impact or experiences. For instance, I've heard many people talk about the "cool factor" of makerspaces, but hardly anyone ever mentions how they are supporting multimodal learning.

I think there is also some danger in overgeneralizing our intentions. For instance, we might designate a zone for "group work" and fill it with tables and chairs. Our stats might indicate that the area is often busy—but is it being well used? Groups have varying requirements. A team in the planning and brainstorming phase has different needs from one that is composing a paper or designing materials. And a team rehearsing a presentation requires something different as well. One size does not fit all.

I observed a related example of this "stuff over substance" when I recently visited a library touting its *classroom of the future*. This elaborate room requires specially trained student assistants to run it. While the space has many bells and whistles and high-resolution displays, many of the librarians avoid the room because the system is too complex. This is a cautionary tale.

When technology takes precedence over people it hinders our capabilities. This is the danger of a technology-centric view.

My suggestion is that instead of focusing on our commons, we shift the conversation to our communities. Our buildings are filled with a large assortment of people who are all there for a multitude of different purposes. Our role becomes similar to that of a city planner—interpreting desires, determining needs, shaping zones, encouraging use and interactions, gathering data, monitoring usage, collecting feedback, adapting on the fly, and basically ensuring that people have what they need in order to thrive.

In this manner our role is not to serve as just learning space managers, but to be community developers. We're building a collection of niches and aim to integrate people with different beliefs, backgrounds, approaches, and opinions into a cohesive and welcoming setting. Libraries are well situated to accommodate these different communities (all with unique needs) while placing them together in a shared experience. Present people with options, facilitate, and inspire: This is the heart and soul of promoting knowledge accessibility.

But just because people are sitting near each other in an open room does not make them a community. For that to happen, they must form a collective identity based on shared perceptions and a common view of their potential. We can create an atmosphere by assembling components (furniture, technologies, supplies, collections, expertise) and some basic rules (guidelines, policies, expectations), but the bonding is up to them. It is not something we can control though we can help optimize the opportunities.

As we consider the future of libraries, perhaps we need a greater investment in understanding the fellowship that occurs between our users. Instead of focusing on technologies and outputs, we focus on interactions and how things influence what people do in our spaces.

Positioning libraries as organic nomadic communities, and more than a place to study, we can then foster intellectual and personal development through the act of bringing people together to share the experience.

Elements of

A sense of belonging to a community has been shown to improve motivation, health, and happiness. We feel less alone, less isolated, more energized. So what about libraries? Our buildings are filled with people, but that doesn't necessarily equate to fostering a nurturing community. How might we better utilize our buildings beyond the aims of productivity?

Just as we've embraced elements from user experience design and ethnography, I can imagine immense value from hiring geographers and community developers as well. Incorporating some of their tools, such as emotional cartography, participatory planning, and asset toolkits, can help us achieve new aspirations.

I see our work evolving from trying to understand how people use a library to how communities form and function within our buildings and across campus. In this way, the library is transformed from study space into a more nurturing habitat.

Here are a few constructs to get us started.

Community development activities should be based on a commitment to the following principles:

Empowerment – increasing the ability of individuals and groups to influence issues that affect them and their communities

Participation – supporting people in taking part in decision-making

Inclusion, equality of opportunity and anti-discrimination – recognizing that some people may need additional support to overcome barriers they face

Self-determination – supporting the right of people to make their own choices

Partnership – recognizing that many agencies can contribute to community development

Community

Some factors that create a sense of community:

Membership—sense of belonging and personal relatedness, personal investment, emotional safety, feeling of acceptance, willingness to sacrifice for the group, identification with the group, sharing common symbols

Influence—mattering, members making a difference in the group, having a say in what happens

Integration and fulfillment of needs—feeling members' needs will be met by resources of the group, rewarding to members, status, group success, shared values, members being willing to help others in the group and receiving help in return

Shared emotional connection—sense of group history, common places and shared events, time together, similar experiences, positive experiences, relationships and bonds between members, shared importance of events and tasks and activities, honors, rewards, and recognition

Dwelling

In many academic and research libraries, a slow shift is occurring across the physical footprint. Increasingly, more of our real estate is being invested in studios, labs, commons spaces, and specialized areas. We may eventually reach a point where the majority of library spaces are filled with people (and technology) instead of stacks (and collections). In this respect, libraries will then become more akin to dwelling places where many people congregate for long periods of time.

This requires several changes. Obviously, the infrastructure will be impacted and we need to work on mechanical systems such as heating and cooling, plumbing, and electrical. But equally as important are the social systems. Organizations centered on collections are different from ones centered on engagement. New skill sets and perceptions will be required by library employees in order to manage and engage across these active environments. Our role shifts from predominantly being the keepers of books to facilitators of interactions and partners with knowledge practices.

I've been inspired by the writings of Scott Bennett (retired University Librarian at Yale), who advocates

libraries will then become more akin to dwelling places where many people congregate for long periods of time

the idea that a good library is one that feels domestic rather than institutional. This notion extends far beyond furniture and technology. A community-oriented library is one where people know the others who are there and generally how things work and what everyone is doing. But taking this further, one's work is also noticed and celebrated.

This communal aspect is something we shouldn't overlook. It's not about aesthetics or even customer service. The goal is to provide facilities offering a wide mixture of encounters and occurrences that over time, and after continued exposure, can generate a change in awareness in how one views, relates to, and engages with the world around one.

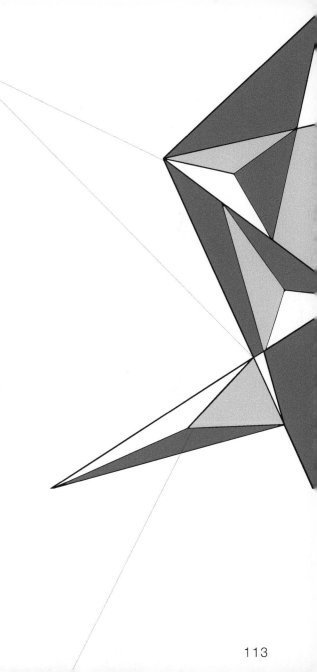

The other thing about the library: There's a group of regular library people who are always here. I've made some really wonderful friendships in the library. There's just kind of a library community of library people doing library things. . . . you get used to seeing specific people every day, and it's really nice. Then sometimes there are little library surprises—like the dog-petting thing or the grilled cheeses, or even some of the programs and lectures. Those things happen and it's like the library is telling you it loves you back.

- an email from a student at Virginia Tech

From Transactions to Transformations

"The local fitness center promotes healthy living and longevity, not the number of clean towels and available treadmills" Yes! #LA101x

Margo Gustina @MargoGustina Feb 23, 2015

This tweet highlights another critical transition—a shift from a transactional mind-set to one that aims to be transformative. It's easy for us to talk about collection size, gate counts, instruction sessions, database searches, the volume of 3D printed objects we produce, or the number of laptops that we lend. We have a deeply rooted service perspective and have become very good at describing the things that we support.

What's challenging, though, is talking about impact. While studies attempt to link library usage with better grades or retention, I'm more interested in a broader mission: improving well-being. Can we use our building to enhance people's lives? This is a powerful mind-set for us to consider. Just as gyms advocate for fitness and provide pathways to a healthy lifestyle, libraries can promote personal and professional development and offer the means to cultivate curiosity and intellectual growth.

A key starting point is shifting focus from a passive view (it's the user's responsibility to figure out what they need) to a more active and engaged approach. Think about how you can become more grounded in your campus infrastructure. Look at the different layers and landscapes surrounding teaching, learning, and research. What's missing? What can be improved? Could we export elements of the library commons model to enhance classrooms, residential spaces, and research buildings?

An active library invests in people's success rather than just the library's success. That's how it measures itself. The objective is to focus on the complex dynamics of the systems around us to better understand the types of engagement or improvements that are necessary. Rather than seeking just to increase our current transactions (answer more reference questions, teach more classes, support more digitalization projects), the goal is to determine barriers that people are facing (beyond just using the library) and then working to reduce roadblocks. Maybe we'll find that students need more writing assistance or math tutors or that faculty could use more help with instructional design. We have to step out of the predefined box of what a library does and open ourselves more holistically to improving the lives of others.

I'm excited about a library that evaluates itself based on how well it partners across campus and its commitment to helping diverse communities flourish.

The Danger of Being Service-Oriented

Libraries pride themselves on offering excellent customer service. We often go out of our way to help faculty and students address their needs. Supporting others' desires is how we derive much of our professional satisfaction.

But as the information landscape shifts all around us, Scott Bennett provides some cautionary thoughts:

The service paradigm can be corrosive for librarians, just as the teaching paradigm is for faculty. Librarians don't want to be clerks serving customers. Like faculty, librarians are people who fell in love with books, learning, technology, and libraries long ago. They want to invite others to share their passion. If we understand learning as not "what's on the test" but as a measure of how well we draw newcomers into communities of knowledge, then promoting student learning means understanding what makes these communities joinable. We need to conceptualize learning correctly. It's not about providing materials (books, databases at your service) but about structuring motive and meaning to nurture the young.

Along these lines, our emphasis becomes encoding environments that welcome and inspire. If our focus is only on service then it restricts the interactions we can create. A service orientation positions us as a commodity rather than a catalyst. It keeps us busy, but passive. My concern is that this leads to a sense of institutionalization, rather than a sense of community and empathy. Ultimately this means performing tasks around compliance. Efficiency and utility, rather than innovation, creativity, or personal meaning, becomes the goal. Service work is too focused on following procedures rather than on being a vehicle for exploration and discovery.

Let's think differently. A professor doesn't just borrow a book, she is deepening her journey as a scholar. A student isn't just working on an assignment, he is stretching his ideas and juggling priorities. Someone doesn't just go to the library; they are intentionally placing themselves in an atmosphere that will bring out the best in them.

I see this transition as a moving away from providing service and instead see us as investing our time, energy, effort, thoughts, resources, and spaces to advance and empower a multitude of diverse communities. Consider ways that you can expand people's capabilities instead of just aiming to satisfy some of their needs.

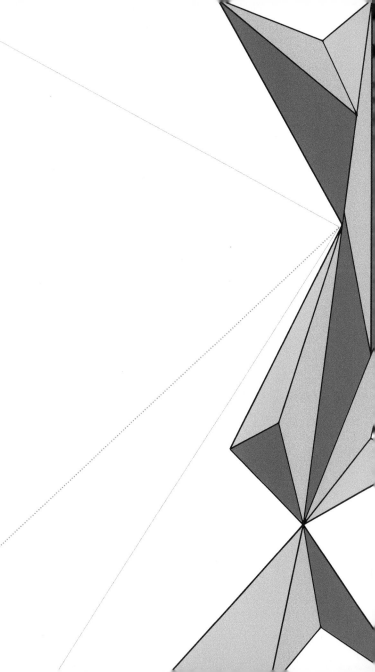

From User-Centered To Learner-Centered

Libraries are increasingly investing in user-centered service models. We are aligning our offerings with the needs and preferences of our campus communities. From our commons areas and collections to our outreach and instruction programs, the overarching objective is making libraries more user-friendly. But is that good enough?

Perhaps we should transition to a learner-centered mindset?

Instead of don't make me think, it becomes make me think more.

Instead of working to make the library more palatable, our emphasis becomes better integration across the learning enterprise.

Instead of aiming to help people become better users of the library, we aspire to partner with them on their learning journey.

These approaches position us more broadly as educators, extending our reach and influence.

My library has started down this path. We are converging around the idea that everyone who enters the building is trying to learn something. By reframing people as learners (instead of patrons, customers, visitors, or users), we move away from just trying to satisfy them and, instead, are trying to enhance their academic progress.

If we embrace this idea of the learner-centered library, then everything we do is pedagogy and all of our employees are instructional designers. Each of us is constantly contributing to the central educational mission and enriching the experience—from how we manage technology to how we engage in classrooms and at service desks, to our signage, events, furniture arrangements, and web content. Every interaction is meaningful.

Build It and They Will Come - So What?

I'm concerned that if all we're doing is swapping out stacks of books for rows of computers, groups of tables, and soft seating that we're becoming vulnerable and remaining passive. Indeed, while libraries may be seeing high numbers of visitors, there is some danger of our effort becoming replicable elsewhere. Others can create reading lounges, collaboration rooms, and makerspaces too.

If you develop areas for people to work in, then they will definitely show up. But is that enough? Is that success?

How does the library remain distinct throughout this transformation? How do we avoid being compared with student centers, study halls, or computer labs?

Perhaps we can learn from startups and tech firms. Research suggests that places like Silicon Valley are successful because of the wide range of specialized services clustered there: advertising, legal support, technical and management consulting, shipping and repair, and engineering support. Simply being there greatly expands one's business capabilities.

Libraries reside at the intersection of disciplines and are well positioned to offer a similar type of ecosystem for scholarly endeavors. This social network is derived from the fusion of expertise residing in our buildings. By crafting our spaces as high-tech, high-touch, co-working environments, we draw diverse communities of people together to tackle complex problems and create expressive forms of media. Students are engaged with each other (and with us) in a dynamic and deliberate setting that emphasizes the usage of data, information, design, writing, coding, presenting, and all their related tools and skills.

Researchers can benefit from our data and publishing services, analytics and metric support, digital library technology development, visualization and design production, ontologists, archivists, and domain experts, and many other specialties. We're in the early stages of creating a new infrastructure—an ecosystem that can propel research, learning, scholarship, entrepreneurialism, social progress, and creativity.

This moves us toward an appealing one-stop-shop model where many niche needs are bundled to allow for a more seamless life cycle. It also increases the possibility of sharing ideas, building connections, and fostering the human spirit.

The commons movement has shown that librarians can build and manage popular destinations and form successful partnerships, but now the next step is connecting people in ways that they can't experience anywhere else on campus.

COMPLEX

ADAPTIVE

SYSTEMS

Dynamic > Static

Learning is nonlinear. So shouldn't our spaces operate in this manner as well?

We may aspire to create a sense of order with predefined user experiences, but instead of always trying to script behaviors, perhaps there is a better approach. The more I have engaged with assessing, designing, and managing learning environments, the more I have come to appreciate them not as physical locations but as complex adaptive systems.

From this point of view, we recognize that all of the things in our environment (the people, the furniture, the technology, and so forth) influence one another. There are constant interactions, interruptions, and interconnections resulting in the adaptation of the environment (and behaviors) in unpredictable and spontaneous ways.

Imagine this: Someone rolls a whiteboard from one side of a room to another. This simple act sets off a kinetic reaction that has a lingering impact for the rest of the day. Because of this placement, other forms of furniture and technologies will be dragged around accordingly. This continuous transfer of people and resources repeatedly reshapes the contour and context of the room.

These small actions, like whiteboard migrations, can happen hundreds of times a day as thousands of students customize the space, influencing everyone and everything around them. As each person responds to one another's movement, the cycle perpetuates itself.

Co-evolution is a core variable here. The commons changes based on how it is used, and therefore people's perceptions and behaviors change too— Who's in it, what they are doing, what's the current condition? As the environment changes, what users do in it also changes. This results in the environment changing again, and the feedback loop continues.

So let's think of it like this. Group A enters the library and pushes a few tables together around a whiteboard. They are working on problem sets for a particular course. In the distance they notice others from their class, and they merge

together to form a super group. They become noisy, and a few students nearby leave to seek a quieter location in neighboring study pods. Others eventually come along to occupy the newly vacated seats. They gauge the activity around them, and they too push tables together to accommodate their own collaborative projects.

Over the course of a day, the room morphs into a setting that supports several large groups. It is loud and rowdy. Eventually this collaborative community dissipates. After that, individuals file into the room and begin pulling apart the table configurations. The space becomes quiet once again, now filed with solo workers.

This (oversimplified) scenario paints a picture of why dynamic settings are more effective than static ones when it comes to spaces intended to support diverse and agile learning outcomes. By recognizing that students and others are involved in rich, complex, and varied tasks, we can best aid them by designing settings that accommodate the constant flow of continuous change. Not only do we allow this to happen, but we also encourage it. The open and rapid transformation of these environments is critical for complex communities. We let them encode the space with the needs that emerge, rather than prescribing a limited range of motion.

You Can't Just Study One Bee

If you want to understand bees, you can't study just a few of them. While you may learn a lot by following one on her journey searching for nectar, that won't enable you to comprehend their communal dynamics.

Bees are social insects always sharing information and opinions. They make decisions together, *democratically*. This includes determining when to start new colonies and where to build more hives, how to distribute workload, and how to protect from threats. They share diverse specialized tasks such as cleaning and building, foraging and guarding. These duties constantly shift as new priorities emerge. And all of these individual activities produce a symphony of coordinated activity. As the environment changes, the bees respond by altering their behaviors accordingly.

A beehive amounts to more than a nest or physical structure; it is a complex adaptive system. I think it would benefit us to think of learning spaces in this manner, too. Libraries are hives of activity where hundreds of people are simultaneously working on a variety of different tasks and yet, all with a sense of harmony.

Likewise, we can't study only a few students and make generalizations about how they use spaces or even about their academic life cycles. They too operate within a communal culture with ever-shifting priorities and stimuli.

It may benefit our observational studies to look at library users collectively instead of individually. For us to appreciate the dynamics involved, we need a better understanding of how the inhabitants interact directly and indirectly while occupying our spaces. Library commons are highly social environments filled with mentoring, co-working, and casual conversation, as well as miscommunications and disagreements.

It could be interesting to dissect this multitude of interactions to understand not just what people are doing but how their actions influence others and the space itself. In this manner, we look at the library as a thriving ecosystem that is constantly morphing. By studying it this way, as an environment with a particular set of cultural norms, we can start down some new paths of inquiry. I can see librarians borrowing from geography and urban planning in order to view our buildings (and the things that happen within them) in a different light.

Play

Trying to force an insight can actually prevent it.

While we might think the best way to solve a problem is to focus head down with minimal distractions, that's not necessarily the best option. This is especially true if it is a complex matter that could benefit from creative connections. If we are isolated and paying attention to only the most relevant details, then our blinders could inhibit potential breakthroughs.

Arguably, letting the mind wander might be the best thing we can do. Big ideas always seem to emerge when people are sidetracked and doing something unrelated to the task at hand. For example, studies have found that most scientists and engineers don't experience epiphanies alone in their labs. Rather, the seeds are planted during random conversations they have with colleagues during meetings, in hallways, and across lunch tables. Social interactions tend to generate ideas and new opportunities for learning.

If you're in an environment that forces you to constantly produce, then you'll likely feel under constant stress. I think this applies to our classrooms and learning spaces, too. Research suggests that when people are comfortable in a casual setting, they actually learn more and feel better about it. Perhaps this is why Google and other innovation-centered companies provide pool tables and Ping-Pong tables for their employees. Not only do they want ideas to cross-pollinate, but they also want the work space to feel fun and energized.

The key theme here is creating a sense of play. Time to be engrossed in activities that offer intrinsic value, providing a break from our typical routines, activates different parts of our brains. From solving puzzles to aerobic movements, play channels us into a different mind-set: one in which we are open to taking risks, testing hunches, and applying our imaginations. It is in these types of atmospheres that creativity and innovation are unlocked and improvisation and problem solving emerge.

An interesting study on playgrounds offers some potential insight. Researchers tested a series of different models from traditional installs (commercially manufactured sets with swings and slides) to adventure parks (with random components such as tires, crates, wooden boards, and buckets). The findings suggest that the playgrounds with predefined activities were less utilized, featured less engaging activities, and were less satisfying to children. On the other hand, the more ambiguous setting stimulated much more activity, inspired creativity, encouraged more co-play and collaboration, and received higher levels of satisfaction.

Why? The main reason appears to be that children had the ability to adapt the environment for any game or situation. The adventure setting also encouraged them to explore the space and to think critically about what resources were available and how to execute their ideas. It stimulated their imaginations and also introduced opportunities for social interactions. Moreover, the open concept provided them with a sense of control and ownership of the environment, allowing them greater attachment and the ability to make it their own.

As we revitalize our library spaces, keeping these attributes of play and ambiguity in mind, it is essential to build environments that are learner-initiated and learner-directed. Like playgrounds, we need libraries that permit cautious risk taking, allow for experimentation, activate working memory, encourage problem solving, encourage the practice of social intelligence, and enhance friendships. Ultimately, we set our sights on spaces that are big, open, multimodal, fun, and welcoming.

the more ambiguous setting stimulated much more activity, inspired creativity, encouraged more co-play and collaboration, and received higher levels of satisfaction

Instruments of Innovation

Are there qualities that help foster innovation? The business literature offers an interesting case study on two companies experimenting with different videoconferencing tools. One provided its employees the top-of-line system, while the other purchased inexpensive webcams with tripods. The results were dramatically different. Those with the high-end system found the equipment too complex and forbidding; they barely used it. The other group, with the lightweight cameras, used them constantly. The portability and ease of use made this option more inviting.

I've seen this sentiment echoed at startup incubators and other innovation-based companies. In fact, I would characterize their settings as playful, rather than high-tech. Plenty of room is available for socialization, productive collusions, and co-working. Their spaces feel less office-like and closer to architecture studios where the ambiance is high-spirited, creative, open, and accessible.

With this example in mind, innovation can't be reduced to a technology checklist. Video walls, 3D printers, digital humanities labs, and the like may garner good press, but they won't transform libraries into innovation hubs. That objective isn't accomplished by gadgets but through forging a culture that gives people permission to experiment and explore.

Perhaps the most essential component in this regard is a sense of malleability. When teams are working on projects or exploring ideas together, they constantly shift between modes of communication: from hushed, to laughter, to excited screams.

Ideation is not linear and our spaces shouldn't be either.

People at work continually move, from standing at whiteboards to hunching over laptops, to crafting prototypes, to sitting back and listening to others. Giving students and faculty the space to discover, diagnose, synthesize, and respond to information as it emerges and evolves is the best way we can support them. We should think of libraries as social apparatuses empowering people to think and act differently than they might elsewhere.

To me, real innovation embraces a sense of rebellion: disrupting the status quo. It's not obtaining million dollar grants, launching companies, or deploying new products, but rather, it's enabling people to make connections that result in them being able to do something new.

an instructor incorporating new literacies

a researcher applying tools from an adjacent discipline

a student designing a new way to articulate a problem

A Great Big Box of Parts

People take inspiration from their surroundings. So why not fill the space with many different options and possibilities? Obviously we want to provide resources to help people be productive, but we should also include some surprises, tiny distractions that can lead to serendipitous encounters.

In my library we introduce a small amount of furniture every year. This keeps the space fresh, and our students are excited to see what we add next. We also fill the commons with artifacts from courses—posters, blueprints, drawings, software, prototypes, and so forth. We want students to be surrounded and inspired by peer output that also offers exposure to interdisciplinary concepts. New ideas are lingering around every corner.

Our aim is to make minor adjustments during the break weeks each semester. We alter the layout of our various commons environments and try new arrangements to see how people react and how they utilize the different tools, technologies, and tables.

I view my library as a great big box of parts. When I select furniture, I look for components that can be mixed and matched. We watch how it's used in order to see what works and to learn what doesn't. Something that doesn't fit in one area could be perfect for another spot. We are always watching for patterns and outliers.

We see how needs emerge and how they are addressed with what is made available; this informs what we buy next or how we shift the layout in the future. Everything is intended to be modular. Pushed. Pulled. Dragged. Stacked. My goal is for students to hack the space and make it their own personal learning environment.

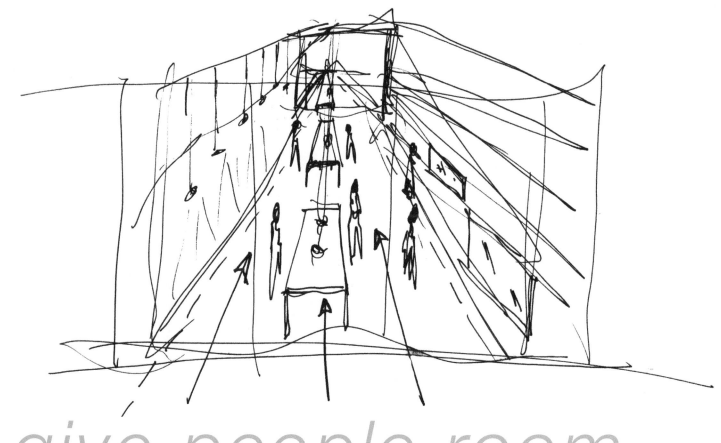

give people room
to make a mess

Perhaps the most radical thing we can do is fill a library with a variety of tables, chairs, and whiteboards—all on wheels. Make sure there is ample electricity and wireless connectivity, and then get out of the way. Let students take it from there.

Neat is the enemy of creativity. If everything is too orderly, too perfect, then it inhibits our imagination. But if the space is a little open-ended (unbounded) and, perhaps, has a touch of chaos, then that frees our thinking about what is possible.

When designing a space, leave some of it unfinished. Don't solve everything; instead, leave room for things to evolve. Ambiguity serves as an invitation. See how the blank space gets used and then let that inform further development. This allows you to uncover unpredictable directions and to address unanticipated needs.

Don't make people ask permission to be innovative. Instead, make everything as radically accessible as possible.

Evolutionary design is healthier than visionary design.

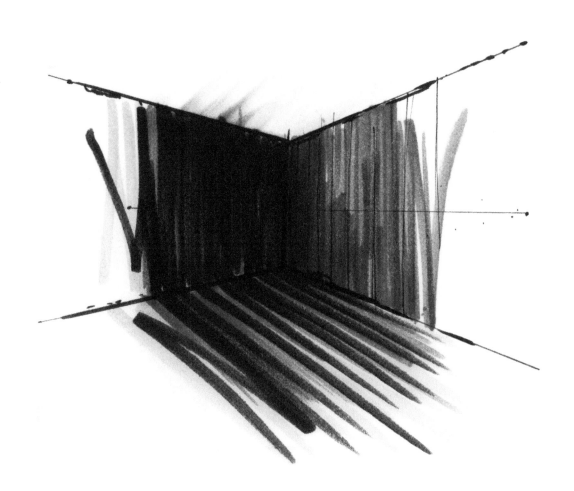

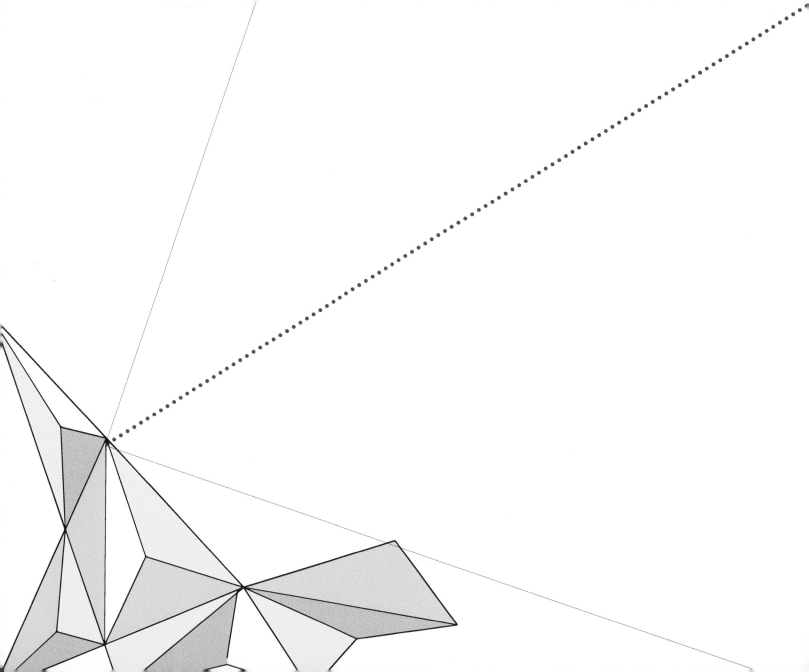

WELL-BEING

WELL-MEANING

Heart

I have often heard libraries referred to as the heart of the university, perhaps serving as a vital (intellectual) organ pumping information out across campus. This metaphor builds around the theme of the circulation of ideas. It could also speak in a poetic or epistemological sense: the love of knowledge, the value of learning, and the epitome of the academic personality.

Are we still the heart today?

Many libraries still use this phrase. Obviously, things have changed. Knowledge formats have evolved and new services have emerged. Our buildings are packed with people, energy, and excitement. Yet, despite all of this activity and how we may view ourselves, I'm curious if students, faculty, staff, and administrators still view libraries as essential.

Perhaps we can reflect on this old metaphor in a different way. Instead of pushing content out across a circulatory pipeline, what if we define the heart differently? Let's think about the heart as a symbol of compassion: an emotional instrument that empowers and enlivens. A heart that is courageous, generous, and gracious. In this manner, the library offers fertile ground for the well-being of the communities that use it.

Yet, maybe in this manner it still does offer a type of circulatory function. Perhaps the ultimate goal of the library is to encourage people to move beyond thinking of themselves and, instead, think more about their impact on others. In this way, a patron's outlook is less about how an experience makes them feel or what the library enables them to accomplish, and, instead, becomes focused on how they can use their skills, experiences, and insights to empower others to feel better about themselves and toward helping others reach for their aspirations. This type of library would truly be the heart of its campus.

I've spent the last decade studying people using library spaces. I have come to believe that they visit libraries because they want to make a change. Maybe it's something small, such as working on homework and adding a new nugget to their knowledge. Or maybe it is something more personally significant, something related to an issue of law, medicine, health, or religion. People go to libraries for new encounters—new people, new ideas, new technologies, new directions, new possibilities. But I think there is also something subconscious happening. We go to libraries to become better versions of ourselves. Each trip is a step forward with self-improvement. We go to figure things out. We go to make sense of situations around us. We go to grow.

What if we made prosperity our core purpose? What if we encoded our spaces to address and advance personal, group, and community well-being? What would libraries look like if they were designed for empathy and to help people thrive in the fullest sense? How might we restructure our personnel and operations if the goal was to improve people's lives? Could we serve as both the intellectual and the compassionate heart for our schools?

Hope

Can environments inspire feelings of hope? If so, then perhaps that is the most powerful attribute that we can encode: *libraries as sources of rejuvenation.* Places that lift the spirit, nourish the mind, and empower self-confidence. Imagine designing that!

A sense of optimism is a vital characteristic that I think we might overlook. Research suggests that first-year students who exhibit a positive outlook are better able to adjust to college. They have fewer symptoms of depression, higher levels of happiness, stronger social networks, and lower attrition rates. Consider how your space might contribute to these outcomes. Libraries are situated as leaders in academic support and places where perseverance is forged and celebrated.

Three core components can foster the sense of possibility:

First, people need goals: a sequence of actions with sufficient value. These objectives must be attainable, yet typically with some degree of difficulty and uncertainty.

Next, people must have pathways: the ability to generate workable routes toward achieving their goals.

The final piece involves agency thinking: the capacity to act and move things forward. This element also provides the motivation to find alternative directions when obstacles emerge. It is such fortitude that prevents us from giving up.

The process is evident around us. For example, a friend of mine joined a fitness competition in order to stay focused on her diet and workout routines. For her it wasn't about winning the contest, but rather, creating conditions to maximize her potential. This motif is present when people commit to running a marathon, hiking the Appalachian Trail, or other physical activities that challenge their endurance. Similarly, when people participate in weekend-long hack-a-thons, they put themselves in a position to push their abilities and create something new. Whether preparing for a long run or a long session of coding, these environments attract communities that are fueled by optimism.

Our buildings, likewise, are filled with communities striving toward different goals. Some may be short-term and task-oriented (prepping for a test, finishing an essay, reading a chapter), while some are long-term (earning a degree, learning a language, making a film). Shifting our focus to helping them achieve these goals (rather than just teaching them to use library resources) opens up new opportunities for our efforts. Our mission becomes the pursuit of understanding—and then engaging however we can to help students and faculty define goals, shape pathways, and activate personal agency.

Furthermore, we can fill our public spaces (and its neural Wi-Fi network) with positivity so that the library not only aligns with productivity, but also nurtures a sense of optimism. In this manner, we aim to transcend supporting research, assignments, and literacies; we also aspire to improve the way people feel about themselves, the way they feel about the work they are doing, and their affinity for the campus as a whole.

Reaching full potential can be realized only when one has the opportunity to take chances. So let's work to open more doors for people, enabling them to pursue new ventures and to challenge themselves to further beyond.

Brain

I began this book with a question: Can physical spaces have an impact on learning experiences? It was retail that initially attracted me with its savvy environments designed to influence our thoughts, feelings, and actions. I wanted to see if I could apply those same concepts to my work in order encourage more concentration, collaboration, creativity, and critical action.

Along the way, I picked up elements from social psychology, neuroscience, and interior design that expanded my thinking. I shifted from wondering how might library buildings be designed better for the future to wondering if they could serve as engines for personal growth and well-being.

The pivotal moment for me was discovering research about brain plasticity. Science suggests that our brains are continuously changing, physically. They are adapting and constantly rewiring based on what we encounter. *What we find changes who we become.* The more we read, the more we exercise, the more we socialize, the more we express ourselves in different modes—all of this meshes to form our perspectives, shape our abilities, determine our limitations, and define who we are. Librarians are not just purveyors of books and journal articles—we're helping people find out who they want to become.

This plasticity has a profound effect on learning. In fact, the very act of learning produces a physical change in our brains. While scientists once believed that brains were fixed, we now know they are constantly morphing. As we interact with the world, our brains respond, making each one of us unique. So, in libraries, we're not just helping people find and use information, we're empowering them to rewire their brains and changing how they relate to and experience the world.

A related insight: Positive emotions in learning are generated in parts of the brain that are used most heavily when students develop their own ideas. In this manner, it benefits us to design pathways for students to own their education. Perhaps a connection can be drawn to the environment in which they learn. If students develop a sense of ownership over their workspace and are able to customize it for various tasks, does this also result in more positive emotions?

Another powerfully influential theme for me was the notion that the way people feel influences what they can do. Creating comfortable environments where people feel cared for and respected maximizes their potential. How do people feel in your library? I've realized that we're not just amassing collections, furniture, and technology; we're building a sense of confidence and achievement across our communities.

If we accept these two ideas (the plasticity of the brain and that supportive spaces equal greater outcomes), then we are facing an enormous responsibility. Our role is nothing short of contributing to the elevation of human consciousness. Or if you prefer a more pragmatic version: The arrangement of the furniture, technology and collections, along with the character of our spaces, has a direct impact on what people are able to accomplish. In this manner, libraries become more than just buildings: They are platforms for immersive intellectual, social, and creative experiences and experiments.

Improving the mind requires more than having access to books, journals, tables, Wi-Fi, or other such items. It requires a more proactive infrastructure with the encoded intention of helping people become better versions of themselves.

Unlocking human potential is not the pursuit of excellence. In fact, I think that has more to do with challenging what is perceived to be excellent. Filling the mind with predetermined knowledge constructs doesn't push our imaginations or spark innovation—it actually just creates limits.

As we redefine the library's programmatic aims accordingly, we can unleash ingenuity by designing opportunities to critique existing opinions and advancing new concepts or different approaches.

I feel that we have a responsibility to help people challenge the status quo while also providing frameworks to improve the world around them.

Perhaps the best thing we can do with our physical spaces is encourage people to learn together. When individuals view themselves as part of a community, they form an unparalleled bond. They become aware of the fullness of problems and issues and grasp the value of different perspectives—they view the diversity of many possible solutions and that in turn strengthens the outcome. Not only are outputs better but personal outcomes thrive as well.

Herein fits the theme of metacognition—our awareness and understanding of our thought processes. Thinking about thinking. Library environments that are active and adaptive can play a huge role in cognitive development. Complex spaces advance our sense-making capacity. As we remake libraries, let's view this as an opportunity for students and faculty to strengthen their spatial literacy and personal agency. By providing them with a multitude of options, they can energize their critical thinking to empower them to determine how they can best learn to accomplish their goals and devise new ones. We are encouraging them to use the library in order to develop greater self-awareness and self-efficacy.

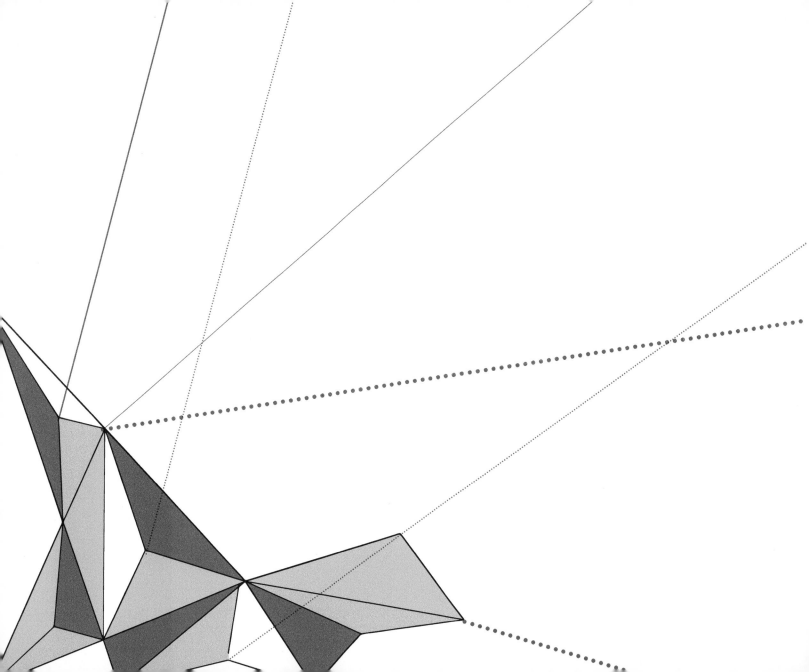

RADICAL
COLLABORATION

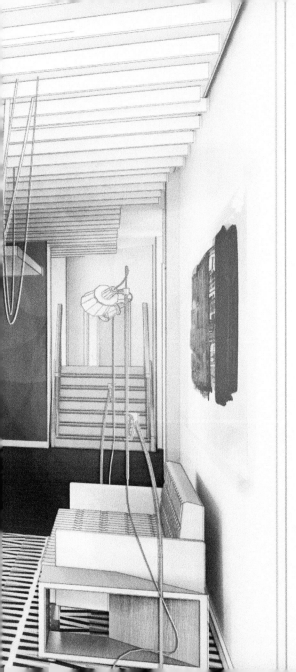

Libraries are complex interrelated environments that foster the generation of new ideas and new ways of creating knowledge.

Being around smart people makes us smarter and more innovative. By clustering near each other, students and faculty foster each other's creative spirit and become more successful.

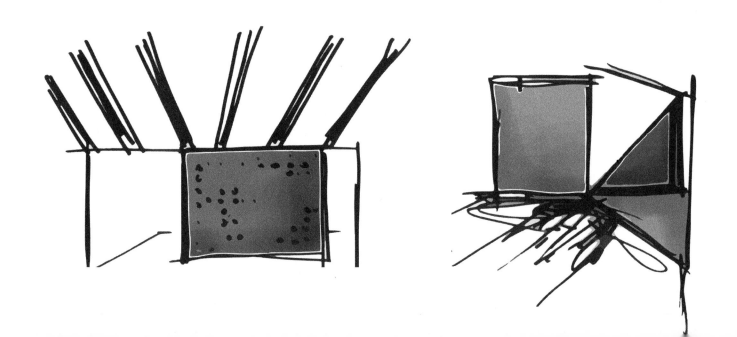

The flow and diffusion of knowledge leads to more creativity, innovation, and knowledge.

Innovation happens when people interact in a fertile environment and their ideas unexpectedly collide to create something that did not exist before.

There is uncertainty about the long-term future of libraries. I've encountered university administrators who openly question the need for library buildings. They view our facilities as prime real estate on campuses starving for more classrooms, labs, and office spaces.

I've also encountered many librarians who are concerned about their legacy. They have spent their entire careers building collections and educating people on how to use them. They see the prominence of these professional values fading.

These are themes that I wanted to explore while assembling this book. How can libraries remain vital and resilient?

When I look to our future, I don't see doom and gloom or obsolescence. Quite the contrary. I think we're entering an era of radical collaboration.

Libraries are experiencing a renaissance. The very construct of knowledge itself—what it is, how it's created, and the ways it gets used—is evolving. Innovative libraries are embracing new responsibilities and pushing the profession in new directions. Today, many of us are more deeply involved across the entire life cycles of teaching and research. We are data curators and pedagogical experts. We build researcher profiles, write software, and construct ontologies. We manage digital projects and digital commons spaces. We partner with student organizations to advocate for social causes. Knowledge needs and practices are becoming increasingly more complex and specialized, and so too are the ways that librarians engage with their communities.

Clearly, our facilities are changing quite dramatically. Not everyone is ready for that. But as print migrates to other formats and we reduce the footprint of our physical stacks, room opens up for new activities and partnerships. Our future will likely involve more people and fewer printed materials, depending on the disciplines we support. The physical copies that we do keep will then become increasingly special: a working collection supplemented, and not supplanted, by electronic resources. Many conversations await us as we determine what tangible media needs to be kept onsite and which materials serve us better in other formats.

Our efforts today are monumental. Each renovation is a small revolution. We're creating something that has never existed before. With each step we are fundamentally changing the very definition of libraries and the act of knowledge creation. Many exciting pathways lie before us. Instead of trying to hold on to what libraries have always been, this is a chance for regeneration.

I have a few final reflections as I consider the future. We should be cautious when saying that libraries are about more than just books. Instead, I have been saying that we're all about books and so much more. Personally, I think it is a better strategy to build upon our past, rather than dismiss it. Books remain a powerful currency. They represent knowledge, and we should continue to celebrate what they symbolize, even if that means more of them are being published digitally. This keeps us grounded in the ideals of reading and thinking. We can build other layers upon that foundation, but always honor the core.

Secondly, we need to think far beyond furniture, technology, and support services. Anyone on your campus can purchase the same things that you can. Everyone can build commons spaces, computer labs, 3D printing services, video walls, and so forth. How does the library remain unique? What do we offer that is different from a student center, a residence hall, or a reading room in an academic building?

Encoding is our key: creating an atmosphere with intended purposes, emotions, and meaning. Give everyone a chance to make it his or her own.

So what's the value of libraries? The answer doesn't hinge on collection analytics, gate counts, reference desk transactions, information literacy post-tests, institutional repository downloads, ROI metrics, retention studies, satisfaction scores or the host of other elements that we typically parade.

I think our value boils down to creating environments that stimulate productive collisions and knowledge spillovers. Learning is messy and we provide a high-touch location for these complex activities and diverse modes of expression. Nurturing the knowledge ecosystem is essential: outfitting our spaces to maximize intellectual and creative potential where people and ideas intermingle. We're in the business of fostering happenstances as well as structured encounters. We bring people and information together so they can create and experience things that otherwise would not have been possible—or even imaginable.

Engaged learning-oriented libraries can engender a better sense of self-awareness and confidence and effect more encounters with global culture and challenging ideas.

Despite the proliferation of digital content, increased globalization, and high mobility, physical spaces have become more important than ever. The best videoconferencing system cannot compete with the intimacy and candor of a group gathering around a whiteboard to diagram ideas. A library increases its value the more it becomes a stage for intellectual play, personal reflection, and creativity. It's a place to find meaning, but also one where we make meaning for ourselves. Libraries will serve as venues of opportunity promoting a higher purpose in life, built to change and embrace adaptive communities.

Do we still need libraries? Actually I think we need more of them. An investment in an active learner-centered library results in more collaboration and introspection. We'll get more art and more algorithms, more poems and more patents. Engagement-centered librarians will help generate more grants, more publications, and more critical analysis. They will help people develop and apply more skills, fluencies, and literacies.

The ultimate value that we create is exploration. Simply put, we help expose and connect students and faculty to new tools, resources, devices, ideas, and people. Engaged learning-oriented libraries can engender a better sense of self-awareness and confidence and effect more encounters with global culture and challenging ideas. And further, our environment may encourage people to rethink and expand their ambitions. I think of this as growing our social infrastructure.

In these types of libraries, students form more friendships, receive more mentorship, and experience more diversity. They feel more supported and nurtured, resulting in greater academic progress, stronger connections with their peers, and a greater affinity with the institute. Broadly speaking, they will be more likely to reach their fuller potential by participating a dynamic learning community.

The campus benefits as well. It becomes more productive, more engaged, more conscientious, and more empowered. We'll hear more courageous conversations and see a healthier, more mindful community. Not only can we expand the boundaries of knowledge, but we can also help unravel elusive or hidden knowledge and preserve existing knowledge so it isn't lost or unusable down the road. Our libraries can serve as the nexus for developing new pedagogical approaches and nurture more active and experiential learning.

Libraries focused on well-being and applied empathy can generate important outcomes. Our society becomes more informed, more energized, more generous, more curious, more ethical, more insightful, and more civically and socially engaged. We'll see more volunteerism, optimism, open-mindedness, perseverance, and philanthropy.

In these libraries, people learn how to learn. They begin to recognize their needs and all the steps in front of them. They are also aware of what they don't know and of when they need help. They develop talent and intuition, while also confronting and overcoming their personal weaknesses and limitations. They apply their creativity as well as analytical reasoning. And perhaps most importantly, they learn to adapt—to do what it takes to navigate tough situations that arise, and to flourish despite unexpected setbacks. Students will develop vital skills for a 21st century economy, while also becoming prepared to fully participate in citizenship and democracy.

Libraries have always been about questions. We naturally want to help people find answers. But that's changing, too. Today we guide them toward finding new questions. We encourage them to challenge existing knowledge constructs. We help them figure out what they need to figure out. Librarians are playing a more significant role with research and learning practices and life cycles— walking alongside students and faculty—departing with them off the well-worn paths and blazing new trails into wilderness in search of new possibilities, findings, and outcomes.

At its heart, the future of library buildings is rooted in stimulating the mind and inviting people to pause, ponder, and produce. Our success will be measured by how well we enable people to ask more questions, better questions, and questions that have never been asked before. Questions that would not be possible to contemplate without the agile knowledge infrastructure and supportive ecosystem that only the library can provide.

As I look further to the future, I envision libraries at the forefront of radical collaborations: playgrounds for new knowledge practices. As the boundaries between disciplines become increasingly fluid, students, scholars, researchers, and others require different types of spaces and encounters. We can fill an important niche by facilitating the intersection of science, technology, policy, and design. We can bring humanists together with computational thinkers to tackle complex problems. Artists together with geographers and agriculturalists to advance sustainability. Medical researchers with economists and engineers to rethink global health. The possibilities of such mashups are limitless, but they require a conscious effort and a well-connected agent with the public good in mind.

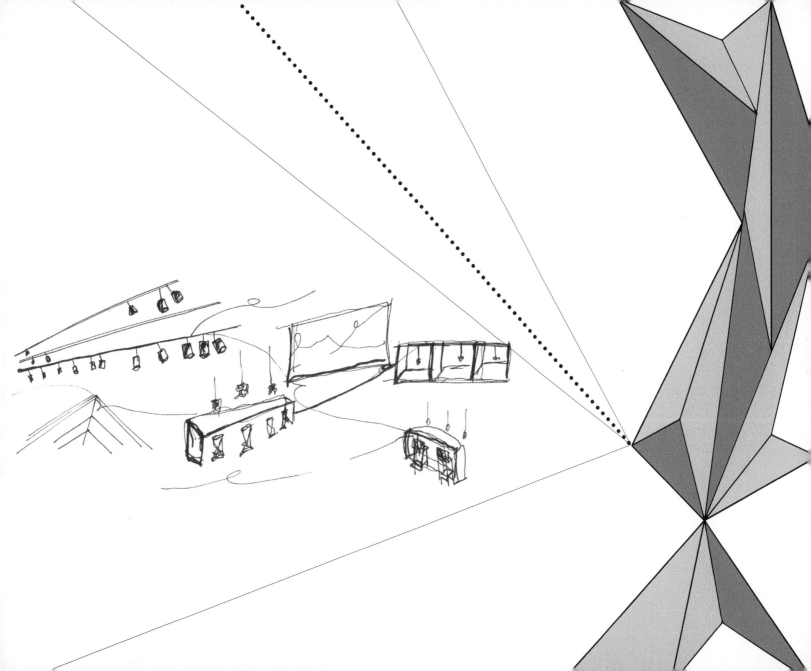

Librarians are uniquely positioned to surmount existing boundaries and to serve as champions of networked innovation and open knowledge. Our professional future is one as partners, collaborators, consultants, and instigators for social, technological, scientific, cultural, and intellectual progress.

The library spaces that we're shaping today are just the start. We have a responsibility to help prepare our communities for a radically different future. We're all facing a world filled with multifaceted social problems and mounting issues, such as health and sustainability. Our professional contribution has to be more than what it is today. We have to transform the way people experience knowledge, and beyond that, how it impacts their thoughts, feelings, decision-making, and actions. Central to our role is helping people feel comfortable with complexity, embrace a serendipitous outlook, and perceive themselves as makers of meaning.

To achieve this ambitious goal we need to design libraries with emergence in mind. Environments must be able to change instantly, rapidly, effortlessly, and dramatically. We need to allow people to converge and build communities around debate, creativity, productivity, reflection, and sharing. Inspire them to encode, self-code, and re-code spaces so they can fill them with aspirations and achievements beyond anything they thought possible.

Notes, References, and Attributions

PROLOGUE

Space transmits culture & body language. Doorley, Scott, Scott Witthoft, and David Kelley. Make space: how to set the stage for creative collaboration. Hoboken, N.J.: John Wiley & Sons, 2012.

Our buildings may be inanimate. Lurie, Alison and Karen Sung. The language of houses: how buildings speak to us. Harrison, New York: Delphinium Books, 2014.

Buildings communicate. Blesser, Barry and Linda-Ruth Salter. Spaces speak, are you listening?: experiencing aural architecture. Cambridge, Mass: MIT Press, 2007.

SWAYED BY OUR SURROUNDINGS

Beautiful/Ugly Rooms. Maslow, Abraham and Norbett Mintz. "Effects of esthetic surroundings." Journal of Psychology 42, no. 2 (1956): 247-254.

Russell, James, and Ulrich Lanius. "Adaptation level and the affective appraisal of environments." *Journal of Environmental Psychology* 4, no. 2 (1984): 119-135.

Space shapes us just as much as we shape it. Brand, Stewart. How buildings learn: what happens after they're built. New York, NY: Viking, 1994.

Learning environments & learning quality

Zull, James. *The art of changing the brain: enriching teaching by exploring the biology of learning.* Sterling, Virginia: Stylus Pub, 2002.

Carey, Benedict. *How we learn: the surprising truth about when, where, and why it happens.* New York: Random House, 2014.

Gallagher, Winifred. *The power of place: how our surroundings shape our thoughts, emotions, and actions.* New York: Poseidon Press, 1993.

Durán-Narucki, Valkiria. "School building condition, school attendance, and academic achievement in New York City Public Schools: a mediation model." *Journal of Environmental Psychology* 28, no. 3 (2008): 278-286.

Strange, Carney and James Banning. *Education by design: creating campus learning environments that work.* San Francisco, CA: Jossey-Bass, 2001.

WHAT MAKES A SPACE A PLACE?

Hiss, Tony. *The experience of place: a new way of looking at and dealing with our radically changing cities and countryside.* New York: Vintage Books/Random House, 1990.

Harrison, Steve, and Paul Dourish. "Re-place-ing space: the roles of place and space in collaborative systems." In Proceedings of the 1996 ACM conference on Computer supported cooperative work, pp. 67-76. ACM, 1996.

Augustin, Sally. *Place advantage: applied psychology for interior architecture.* Hoboken, N.J.: John Wiley & Sons, 2009.

Canter, David. *The psychology of place.* London: Architectural Press, 1977.

FROM DICHOTOMY TO ECOLOGY

This section was inspired by conversations with Tara Patterson.

Cain, Susan. Quiet: *the power of introverts in a world that can't stop talking.* New York: Crown Publishers, 2012.

Evans, Gary and Richard Wener. "Crowding and personal space invasion on the train: please don't make me sit in the middle." *Journal of Environmental Psychology* 27, no. 1 (2007): 90-94.

Lankes, David. *Expect more: demanding better libraries for today's complex world.* Jamesville, NY: Riland Publishing, 2012.

KNOWLEDGE SPILLOVERS

Moretti, Enrico. *The new geography of jobs.* Boston: Houghton Mifflin Harcourt, 2012.

ATTACHMENT

Community

Mannarini, Terri, Stefano Tartaglia, Angela Fedi, and Katiuscia Greganti. "Image of neighborhood, self-image and sense of community." *Journal of Environmental Psychology* 26, no. 3 (2006): 202-214.

Lewicka, Maria. "Ways to make people active: The role of place attachment, cultural capital, and neighborhood ties." *Journal of Environmental Psychology* 25, no. 4 (2005): 381-395.

Young, Anne, Anne Russell, and Jennifer Powers. "The Sense of Belonging to a neighbourhood: can it be measured and is it related to health and well being in older women?" *Social Science & Medicine* 59, no. 12 (2004): 2627-2637.

Lewicka, Maria. "What makes neighborhood different from home and city? Effects of place scale on place attachment." *Journal of Environmental Psychology* 30, no. 1 (2010): 35-51.

Hikers

Tsaur, Sheng-Hshiung, Ying-Wen Liang, and Szu-Chun Weng. "Recreationist-environment fit and place attachment." *Journal of Environmental Psychology* 40 (2014): 421-429.

Residential Learning Communities

Curtin, Meredith. "The effects of membership in residential learning communities." *Journal of College and Character* 2, no. 11 (2001).

Pike, Gary. "The effects of residential learning communities and traditional residential living arrangements on educational gains during the first year of college." *Journal of College Student Development* 40, no 33 (1999): 269-284.

Chow, Kenny and Mick Healey. "Place attachment and place identity: first-year undergraduates making the transition from home to university." *Journal of Environmental Psychology* 28, no. 4 (2008): 362-372.

Shushok, Frank, T. Laine Scales, Rishi Sriram, and Vera Kidd. "A tale of three campuses: Unearthing theories of residential life that shape the student learning experience." *About Campus* 16, no. 3 (2011): 13-21.

Sriram, Rishi and Frank Shushok. "Exploring the effect of a residential academic affairs-student affairs partnership: The first year of an engineering and computer science living-learning center." *Journal of College & University Student Housing* 36, no. 2 (2010): 68-81.

WHEN A CHAIR IS MORE THAN A PLACE TO SIT

Places enhance our moods

Gallagher, Winifred. *The power of place: how our surroundings shape our thoughts, emotions, and actions.* New York: Poseidon Press, 1993.

SPACE IMPARTS ACTION

Lewin, Kurt. "Defining the 'field at a given time.'" *Psychological Review* 50, no. 3 (1943): 292-310.

Burnes, Bernard and Bill Cooke. "Kurt Lewin's field theory: a review and re-evaluation." *International Journal of Management Reviews* 14, no. 4 (2013): 408 – 425.

Austin, Jim. "B=f(p,e)." Assessed November 13, 2015. https://www.linkedin.com/pulse/20140620122441-31945425-b-f-p-e

PROGRAMMABLE SPACE

I am grateful to Crit Stuart, Bob Fox, and Charlie Bennett for our many rambling conversations about "programming the commons" at the Georgia Tech Libraries.

Barden, Phil. *Decoded: the science behind why we buy.* Chichester, West Sussex: John Wiley & Sons, 2013.

Pfeiffer, Toni Sachs. "Behaviour and interaction in built space." *Built Environment* (1978-) (1980): 35-50.

Cafeterias

Brian Wansink, David Just, and Joe Mckendry. "Lunch line redesign: op-chart." *New York Times*. Accessed November 13, 2015. http://www.nytimes.com/interactive/2010/10/21/opinion/20101021_Oplunch.html

Wansink, Brian. Slim by design: mindless eating solutions for everyday life. New York: William Morrow, 2014.

Choice Architects

Thaler, Richard and Cass Sunstein. *Nudge: improving decisions about health, wealth, and happiness.* New Haven, Conn: Yale University Press, 2008.

RETAIL (EXCHANGE)

Robinson, Jennifer and J. A. Hartenfeld. *The farmers' market book: growing food, cultivating community.* Bloomington, Indiana: Indiana University Press, 2007.

Bernstein, William. A splendid exchange: *how trade shaped the world*. New York: Grove, 2009.

Lindström, Martin. *Buyology: the new science of why we buy.* New York: Currency Doubleday, 2008.

Burke, Raymon. "Retail shoppability: a measure of the world's best stores." *Future Retail Now* 40 (2005): 206-219.

DeJean, Joan. *The essence of style: how the French invented high fashion, fine food, chic cafés, style, sophistication, and glamour.* New York: Simon and Schuster, 2007.

PERSUASIVE SPACE

Underhill, Paco. *Why we buy: the science of shopping.* New York: Simon & Schuster, 1999.

Plunkett, Drew and Olga Reid. *Detail in contemporary retail design.* London: Laurence King, 2012.

Sorensen, Herb. *Inside the mind of the shopper: the science of retailing.* Upper Saddle River, N.J.: Wharton School Publishing, 2009.

Barden, Phil. *Decoded: the science behind why we buy.* Chichester, West Sussex: John Wiley & Sons, 2013.

Weishar, Joseph. *Design for effective selling space.* New York: McGraw-Hill, 1992.

Miles, Steven. *Spaces for consumption: pleasure and placelessness in the post-industrial city.* Los Angeles: SAGE, 2010.

Gladwell, Malcolm. *"The science of shopping."* The New Yorker 4, no. 11 (1996): 66-75.

THE MOST IMPORTANT THING

Hospitals

Andrade, Cláudia and Ann Sloan Devlin. "Stress reduction in the hospital room: applying Ulrich's Theory of supportive design." *Journal of Environmental Psychology* 41 (2015): 125-134.

Fornara, Ferdinando, Marino Bonaiuto, and Mirilia Bonnes. "Perceived hospital environment quality indicators: a study of orthopaedic units." *Journal of Environmental Psychology* 26, no. 4 (2006): 321-334.

Underhill, Paco. *Why we buy: the science of shopping.* New York: Simon & Schuster, 1999.

Sorensen, Herb. *Inside the mind of the shopper: the science of retailing.* Upper Saddle River, N.J.: Wharton School Publishing, 2009.

Snodgrass Jacalyn, James Russell, and Lawrence Ward. "Planning, mood, and place-liking." *Journal of Environmental Psychology* 8, no. 3 (1988): 209-222.

Martineau, Pierre. "The personality of the retail store." *Harvard Business Review* 36 (1958): 47-55.

VOCABULARY

O'Shea, Linda, Chris Grimley, and Mimi Love. *Interior design reference & specification book: everything interior designers need to know every day* Gloucester, Mass: Rockport Publishers, 2013.

Bell, Judith and Kate Ternus. *Silent selling: best practices and effective strategies in visual merchandising.* New York City, NY: Fairchild Publications, 2006.

MERCHANDISING

Ebster, Claus and Marion Garaus. *Store design and visual merchandising creating store space that encourages buying.* New York: Business Expert Press, 2011.

Gorman, Greg. *Visual merchandising and store design workbook.* New York: ST Media Group International, 1996.

Bell, Judith and Kate Ternus. *Silent selling: best practices and effective strategies in visual merchandising.* New York City, NY: Fairchild Publications, 2006.

Pegler, Martin. *Visual merchandising and display.* New York: Fairchild Books, 2012.

VISUAL CUES

Rogers, Yvonne, Jenny Preece, and Helen Sharp. *Interaction design: beyond human-computer interaction.* Chichester: Wiley, 2015.

Weishar, Joseph. *Design for effective selling space.* New York: McGraw-Hill, 1992.

Burke, Raymon. *"Retail shoppability: a measure of the world's best stores."* Future Retail Now 40 (2005): 206-219.

THE SOUL OF A SPACE

Underhill, Paco. *The call of the mall.* New York: Simon & Schuster, 2004.

Sorensen, Herb. *Inside the mind of the shopper: the science of retailing.* Upper Saddle River, N.J.: Wharton School Publishing, 2009.

Miles, Steven. *Spaces for consumption: pleasure and placelessness in the post-industrial city.* Los Angeles: SAGE, 2010.

Mehta, Ravi, Rui Juliet Zhu, and Amar Cheema. "Is noise always bad? Exploring the effects of ambient noise on creative cognition." *Journal of Consumer Research* 39, no. 4 (2012): 784-799.

Stapel, Diederik, Janneke Joly, and Siegwart Lindenberg. "Being there with others: How people make environments norm-relevant." *British Journal of Social Psychology* 49, no. 1 (2010): 175-187.

Turley, Lou. "How 'atmospherics' can differentiate retail outlets." *European Business Forum* 4 (2000): 49-52.

Turley, Lou and Jean-Charles Chebat. "Linking retail strategy, atmospheric design and shopping behaviour." *Journal of Marketing Management* 18, no. 1-2 (2002): 125-144.

AUDIT YOUR ATMOSPHERE

Audit Elements

Turley, Lou and Ronald Milliman. "Atmospheric effects on shopping behavior: a review of the experimental evidence." *Journal of Business Research* 49, no. 2 (2000): 193-211.

COLOR

Wilmes, Barbara, Lauren Harrington, Patty Kohler-Evans, and Davis Sumpter. "Coming to our senses: incorporating brain research findings into classroom instruction." *Education* 28 no.4 (2008): 659-666.

Pile, John. *Color in interior design*. New York: McGraw-Hill, 1997.

Johnson, Heidi and Jennifer Maki. "Color sense." *American School & University* 81, no. 13 (2009): 143-145.

A POINT OF VIEW

Traub, Marvin and Tom Teicholz. *Like no other store: the Bloomingdale's legend and the revolution in American marketing.* New York: Times Books. 1993.

Zukin, Sharon. *Point of purchase: how shopping changed American culture.* New York: Routledge, 2004.

Burkhart, Jesse. "The science of retail: experts explain how to tap into the psyche of shoppers." *Home Accents Today.* March 1, 2012. Accessed on November 13, 2015. https://www.highbeam.com/doc/1G1-318752108.html

Sorensen, Herb. *Inside the mind of the shopper: the science of retailing.* Upper Saddle River, N.J.: Wharton School Publishing, 2009.

NURTURING THE SCHOLARLY IMPULSE

Kacen, Jacqueline, James Hess, and Doug Walker. "Spontaneous selection: the influence of product and retailing factors on consumer impulse purchases." *Journal of Retailing and Consumer Services* 19, no. 6 (2012): 578-588.

Mohan, Geetha, Bharadhwaj Sivakumaran, and Piyush Sharma. "Impact of store environment on impulse buying behavior." *European Journal of Marketing* 47, no. 10 (2013): 1711-1732.

IS IT WHAT YOU THOUGHT IT WOULD BE?

Sirgy, Joseph, Dhruv Grewal, and Tamara Mangleburg. "Retail Environment, Self-Congruity, and Retail Patronage." *Journal of Business Research* 49, no. 2 (2000): 127-138.

O'cass, Aron and Debra Grace. "Understanding the Role of Retail Store Service in Light of Self-image–store Image Congruence." *Psychology & Marketing* 25, no 5 (2008): 521-537.

Sorensen, Herb. *Inside the mind of the shopper: the science of retailing.* Upper Saddle River, N.J.: Wharton School Publishing, 2009.

Lin, Ingrid. "Evaluating a servicescape: The effect of cognition and emotion." *International Journal of Hospitality Management* 23, no. 2 (2004): 163-178.

Burkhart, Jesse. "The science of retail: experts explain how to tap into the psyche of shoppers." *Home Accents Today.* March 1, 2012. Accessed on November 13, 2015. https://www.highbeam.com/doc/1G1-318752108.html

PRIMED FOR SUCCESS

Stapel, Diederik, Janneke Joly, and Siegwart Lindenberg. "Being there with others: how people make environments norm-relevant." *British Journal of Social Psychology* 49 (2010): 175-187.

Thaler, Richard and Cass Sunstein. *Nudge: improving decisions about health, wealth, and happiness.* New Haven, Conn: Yale University Press, 2008.

Pink, Daniel. *Drive: the surprising truth about what motivates us.* New York: Riverhead Books, 2012.

Kerr, John, and Paul Tacon. "Psychological responses to different types of locations and activities." *Journal of Environmental Psychology* 19, no. 3 (1999): 287-294.

STORE-WITHIN-A-STORE

Kinshuk, Jerath and John Zhang "Store within a store." *Journal of Marketing Research*: 47, no 4 (2010): 748-763.

AWAY FROM THE DESK

Spector, Robert and Patrick McCarthy. *The Nordstrom way to customer service excellence: a handbook for implementing great service in your organization.* Hoboken, N.J.: John Wiley & Sons, 2005.

OMNI CHANNEL

Piotrowicz, Wojciech and Richard Cuthbertson. "Introduction to the special issue information technology in retail: toward omnichannel retailing." International *Journal of Electronic Commerce* 18, no. 4 (2014): 5-16.

Brynjolfsson, Erik, Yu Jeffrey Hu, and Mohammad Rahman. "Competing in the age of omnichannel retailing." *MIT Sloan Management Review* 54, no. 4 (2013): 23-29.

Dickenson, Susan. "Special Report: the future of retail." *Home Accents Today,* March 1, 2013: 28-33.

Warby Parker

Clifford, Stephanie. "Once proudly web only, shopping sites hang out real shingles." *New York Times* 18 (2012): 5.

Indvik, Lauren. "SoHo gives a glimpse of retail's future" *Mashable.com.* June 9, 2013. Accessed on November 13, 2015. http://mashable.com/2013/06/09/retail-store-future/#gng3tgpO8EqR

CURATING BEHAVIORS

Farris, Paul. *Marketing metrics: the definitive guide to measuring marketing performance.* Upper Saddle River, N.J.: FT Press, 2010.

Cox, Emmett. *Retail analytics the secret weapon.* Hoboken, N.J.: Wiley, 2012.

Matthews, Joseph. *Library assessment in higher education.* Westport: Libraries Unlimited, 2007.

Hernon, Peter and Robert Dugan. Outcomes assessment in your library. Chicago: American Library Association, 2002.

Lewis, Robin and Michael Dart. *The new rules of retail: competing in the world's toughest marketplace.* New York, NY: Palgrave Macmillan, 2010.

Stephens, Doug. *The retail revival reimagining business in the new age of consumerism.* Toronto: Wiley & Sons, 2013.

Snodgrass Jacalyn, James Russell, and Lawrence Ward. "Planning, mood, and place-liking." *Journal of Environmental Psychology* 8, no. 3 (1988): 209-222.

Mohan, Geetha, Bharadhwaj Sivakumaran, and Piyush Sharma. "Store environment's impact on variety seeking behavior." *Journal of Retailing and Consumer Services* 19, no. 4 (2012): 419-428.

Pfeiffer, Toni Sachs. "Behaviour and interaction in built space." *Built Environment* (1978-) (1980): 35-50.

PERSONALIZATION

Kepron, David. *Retail (r)evolution: why creating right-brained stores will shape the future of shopping in a digitally driven world.* New York: ST Media Group International, 2014.

Dickenson, Susan. "Special Report: the future of retail." *Home Accents Today,* March 1, 2013: 28-33.

Target

Duhigg, Charles. "How companies learn your secrets." *New York Times Magazine.* February 16. 2012.

RESPONSIVE SPACE

Peterson, Clarissa. *Learning responsive Web design: a beginner's guide.* New York: O'Reilly Media, 2014.

Weishar, Joseph. *Design for effective selling space.* New York: McGraw-Hill, 1992.

Bentley, Ian. *Responsive environments: a manual for designers.* London: Architectural Press, 1985.

DESIGN CONCEPTS

I used virtual reality headgear as an example but you could apply this practice to anything such as prototyping tools, feminist pedagogy or service learning projects. The purpose is to point out the distinction between the types of interactions and the different levels of support or engagement within each concept design.

CONCEPT 4

Whitaker, Jan. *The department store: history, design, display.* London: Thames & Hudson, 2011.

Lisicky, Michael J. *Wanamaker's: meet me at the eagle.* Charleston, SC: History Press, 2010.

ENCODING ENVIRONMENTS

Sime, Jonathan. "Creating places or designing spaces?" *Journal of Environmental Psychology* 6, no 1 (1986): 49-63.

Barden, Phil. *Decoded: the science behind why we buy.* Chichester, West Sussex: John Wiley & Sons, 2013.

Awan, Nishat, Tatjana Schneider, and Jeremy Till. *Spatial agency: other ways of doing architecture.* Abingdon, England: Routledge, 2011.

Walter, Eugene. *Placeways: a theory of the human environment.* Chapel Hill: University of North Carolina Press, 1988.
De Kerckhove, Derrick. The architecture of intelligence. Basel: Birkhäuser, 2001.

Bentley, Ian. *Responsive environments: a manual for designers.* London: Architectural Press, 1985.

Staats, Henk and Terry Hartig. "Alone or with a friend: a social context for psychological restoration and environmental preferences." *Journal of Environmental Psychology* 24 (2004): 199-211.

Csikszentmihalyi, Mihaly. *Flow: the psychology of optimal experience.* New York: Harper & Row, 1990.

Johnson, Steven. *Emergence: the connected lives of ants, brains, cities, and software.* New York: Scribner, 2001.

Cattell, Vicky, Nick Dines, Wil Gesler, and Sarah Curtis. "Mingling, observing, and lingering: everyday public spaces and their implications for well-being and social relations." *Health & Place* 14, no. 3 (2008): 544-561.

Nova, Nicolas. "A review of how space affords socio-cognitive processes during collaboration." *PsychNology* 3, no. 2 (2005): 118-148.

Russell, James, and Ulrich Lanius. "Adaptation level and the affective appraisal of environments." *Journal of Environmental Psychology* 4, no. 2 (1984): 119-135.

BUT CAN WE ENCODE?

Manzo, Lynne. "For better or worse: exploring multiple dimensions of place meaning." *Journal of Environmental Psychology* 25 (2005): 67-86.

Day, Linda. "Placemaking by design: fitting a large new building into a historic district." *Environment and Behavior* 24 (1992): 326-346.

Auburn, Timothy and Rebecca Barnes. "Producing place: a neo-schutzian perspective on the 'psychology of place'." *Journal of Environmental Psychology 26* (2006): 38-50.

Mazumdar, Sanjoy. "How programming can become counterproductive: an analysis of approaches to programming." *Journal of Environmental Psychology 12*, no. 1 (1992): 65-91.

Proshansky, Harold, William Ittelson, and Leanne Rivlin. *Environmental psychology: people and their physical settings.* New York: Holt, Rinehart and Winston, 1976.

Kerr, John, and Paul Tacon. "Psychological responses to different types of locations and activities." *Journal of Environmental Psychology 19*, no. 3 (1999): 287-294.

TRANSITION 1

Third places.

Oldenburg, Ray. *The great good place: cafés, coffee shops, bookstores, bars, hair salons, and other hangouts at the heart of a community.* New York: Marlowe, 1999.

Magnet places

Farrell, Michael. *Collaborative circles: friendship dynamics & creative work.* Chicago: University of Chicago Press, 2001.

Shenk, Joshua Wolf. *Powers of two: finding the essence of innovation in creative pairs.* New York, New York: Houghton Mifflin Harcourt, 2015.

Neural Wi-Fi

Crutchley, Lee. "Neural Wi-Fi." July 30, 2014. Accessed November 13, 2015. http://leecrutchley.co.uk/blog/neural-wifi

Shenk, Joshua Wolf. *Powers of two: finding the essence of innovation in creative pairs.* New York, New York: Houghton Mifflin Harcourt, 2015.

Goleman, Daniel. *Social intelligence: the new science of human relationships.* New York: Bantam Books, 2006.

Stapel, Diederik, Janneke Joly, and Siegwart Lindenberg. "Being there with others: How people make environments norm-relevant." *British Journal of Social Psychology 49,* no. 1 (2010): 175-187.

TRANSITION 2

Block, Peter. *Community the structure of belonging.* San Francisco: Berrett-Koehler Publishers, 2008.

Hughes, Patricia. *Gracious space: working better together.* Seattle, WA: Center for Ethical Leadership, 2004.

Kretzmann, John and John McKnight. *Building communities from the inside out: a path toward finding and mobilizing a community's assets.* Evanston, Ill: Institute for Policy Research, Northwestern University, 1993.

Jacobs, Jane. *The death and life of great American cities.* Vintage, 1961.

Lankes, David. *Expect more: demanding better libraries for today's complex world.* Jamesville, NY: Riland Publishing, 2012.

ELEMENTS OF COMMUNITY

Principles

Scottish Executive. *Working and learning together to build stronger communities.* Edinburgh, Scotland: Crown, 2004. http://www.gov.scot/Resource/Doc/47210/0028730.pdf

Factors

Spinks, David. "The psychology of communities – 4 factors that create a "sense of community" *The Community Manager.* November 19, 2013. http://thecommunitymanager.com/2013/11/19/the-psychology-of-communities-4-factors-that-create-a-sense-of-community/

DWELLING

Seamon, David and Robert Mugerauer. *Dwelling, place, and environment: towards a phenomenology of person and world.* Malabar, Fla: Krieger Publishing, 2000.

Bennett, Scott. *Libraries designed for learning.* Washington, D.C.: Council on Library and Information Resources, 2003. http://www.clir.org/pubs/abstract/reports/pub122

Bennett, Scott. "The information or the learning commons: which will we have?" *Journal of Academic Librarianship 34*, no. 3 (2008): 183-185.

TRANSITION 3

Margo Gustina @MargoGustina Feb 23, 2015 "The local fitness center promotes healthy living and longevity, not the number of clean towels and available treadmills" Yes! #LA101x Accessed via Twitter on November 13, 2015. https://twitter.com/MargoGustina/status/569947481443868672

Bettencourt, Lance. *Service innovation: how to go from customer needs to breakthrough services.* New York: McGraw-Hill, 2010.

THE DANGER OF BEING SERVICE-ORIENTED

Bennett, Scott. "Righting the balance." In *Library as place: rethinking roles, rethinking space,* edited by Geoffrey Freeman, 10-24. Washington, D.C.: Council on Library and Information Resources, 2005.

Bennett, Scott. *Libraries designed for learning.* Washington, D.C.: Council on Library and Information Resources, 2003. http://www.clir.org/pubs/abstract/reports/pub122

Clarke, Ian and Ruth Schmidt. "Beyond the Servicescape." *Journal of Retailing and Consumer Services 2,* no. 3 (1995): 149-162.

TRANSITION 4

Don't make me think.

Krug, Steve. *Don't make me think!: a common sense approach to Web usability.* Berkeley, Calif: New Riders, 2006.

Fink, L. Dee. *Creating significant learning experiences: an integrated approach to designing college courses.* San Francisco, Calif: Jossey-Bass, 2003.

Bransford, John, Ann Brown, and Rodney Cocking. *How people learn: brain, mind, experience, and school.* National Academy Press, 1999.

Hartson, Rex and Pardha Pyla. *The UX book: process and guidelines for ensuring a quality user experience.* Burlington, Mass: Morgan Kaufmann, 2012.

Hattie, John and Gregory Yates. *Visible learning and the science of how we learn.* London: Routledge, 2014.

Barr, Robert and John Tagg. "From teaching to learning: a new paradigm for undergraduate education." *Change.* 27, no. 6 (1995): 13 – 25.

Shor, Ira. *When students have power: negotiating authority in a critical pedagogy.* Chicago: University of Chicago Press, 1996.

Christensen, Clayton, Michael Horn, and Curtis Johnson. *Disrupting class: how disruptive innovation will change the way the world learns.* New York: McGraw-Hill, 2011.

Davidson, Cathy. *Now you see it: how technology and brain science will transform schools and business for the 21st century.* New York: Penguin, 2011.

I'm thankful to Lauren Pressley and Rebecca Miller for our many conversations about pedagogy and learning.

BUILD IT AND THEY WILL COME-SO WHAT?

Moretti, Enrico. *The new geography of jobs.* Boston: Houghton Mifflin Harcourt, 2012.

Lansdale, Mark, Jennifer Parkin, Simon Austin, and Thom Baguley. "Designing for interaction in research environments: a case study." *Journal of Environmental Psychology* 31, no. 4 (2011): 407-420.

Nova, Nicolas. "A review of how space affords socio-cognitive processes during collaboration." *PsychNology* 3, no. 2 (2005): 118-148.

DYNAMIC > STATIC

Miller, John and Scott Page. *Complex adaptive systems an introduction to computational models of social life.* Princeton, N.J.: Princeton University Press, 2007.

Johnson, Steven. *Emergence: the connected lives of ants, brains, cities, and software.* New York: Scribner, 2001.

Urhahn Urban Design (Firm). *The spontaneous city.* Amsterdam: BIS Publishers, 2011.

YOU CAN'T STUDY JUST ONE BEE

Seeley, Thomas. *Honeybee democracy.* Princeton, N.J.: Princeton University Press, 2010.

Seeley, Thomas. *Honeybee ecology: a study of adaptation in social life.* Princeton, N.J.: Princeton University Press, 1985.

Tautz, Ju and David Sandeman. *The buzz about bees: biology of a superorganism.* Berlin: Springer, 2008.

PLAY

Solomon, Susan. *The science of play: how to build playgrounds that enhance children's development.* Hanover: University Press of New England, 2014.

Ozdemir, Aydin and Oguz Yilmaz. "Assessment of outdoor school environments and physical activity in ankara's primary schools." *Journal of Environmental Psychology* 28, no. 3 (2008): 287-300.

Johnson, Steven. *Where good ideas come from: the natural history of innovation.* New York: Riverhead Books, 2010.

Shor, Ira. *When students have power: negotiating authority in a critical pedagogy.* Chicago: University of Chicago Press, 1996.

Cattell, Vicky, Nick Dines, Wil Gesler, and Sarah Curtis. "Mingling, observing, and lingering: everyday public spaces and their implications for well-being and social relations." *Health & Place* 14, no. 3 (2008): 544-561.

Forcing insight.

Lehrer, Jonah. "The eureka hunt." *The New Yorker.* July 28, 2008.

Playground comparisons.

Proshansky, Harold, William Ittelson, and Leanne Rivlin. *Environmental psychology: people and their physical settings.* New York: Holt, Rinehart and Winston, 1976.

INSTRUMENTS OF INNOVATION

Videoconferencing . Harrison, Steve, and Paul Dourish. "Re-place-ing space: the roles of place and space in collaborative systems." In *Proceedings of the 1996 ACM conference on Computer supported cooperative work*, pp. 67-76. ACM, 1996.

Lansdale, Mark, Jennifer Parkin, Simon Austin, and Thom Baguley. "Designing for interaction in research environments: a case study." *Journal of Environmental Psychology* 31, no. 4 (2011): 407-420.

Oksanen, Kaisa and Pirjo Ståhle. "Physical environment as a source for innovation: investigating the attributes of innovative space." *Journal of Knowledge Management* 17, no. 6 (2013): 815-827.

Moultrie, James, Mikael Nilsson, Marcel Dissel, Udo-Ernst Haner, Sebastiaan Janssen, and Remko Van der Lugt. "Innovation spaces: towards a framework for understanding the role of the physical environment in innovation." *Creativity and Innovation Management* 16, no. 1 (2007): 53-65.

Radically Accessible

Doorley, Scott, Scott Witthoft, and David Kelley. *Make space: how to set the stage for creative collaboration*. New Jersey: John Willey & Sons, 2012.

Evolutionary/visionary

Brand, Stewart. *How buildings learn: what happens after they're built*. New York, NY: Viking, 1994.

HOPE

Snyder, C. R., Kevin Rand, and David Sigmon. "Hope theory: A member of the positive psychology family." In *Handbook of positive psychology*, edited by C. R Snyder and Shane Lopez, 257-276. Oxford, England: Oxford University Press, 2002.

BRAIN

I'm thankful to Lauren Pressley and Rebecca Miller for our many conversations about metacognition and epistemology.

Hattie, John and Gregory Yates. *Visible learning and the science of how we learn*. London: Routledge, 2014.

Zull, James. *The art of changing the brain: enriching teaching by exploring the biology of learning*. Sterling, Va: Stylus Pub, 2002.

Carey, Benedict. *How we learn: the surprising truth about when, where, and why it happens*. New York: Random House, 2014.

Crawford, Fred and Ryan Mathews. *The myth of excellence: why great companies never try to be the best at everything*. New York, N.Y.: Crown Pub, 2001.

Durán-Narucki, Valkiria. "School building condition, school attendance, and academic achievement in New York City Public Schools: a mediation model." *Journal of Environmental Psychology* 28, no. 3 (2008): 278-286.

Davidson, Cathy. *Now you see it: how technology and brain science will transform schools and business for the 21st century*. New York: Penguin, 2011.

What we find changes who we become.

Morville, Peter. *Ambient findability: what we find changes who we become*. Sebastopol, CA: O'Reilly Media, 2005.

RADICAL COLLABORATION

The spirit of this section was inspired by tours of startup incubators, technology companies, R&D offices, medical labs, design studios, artist studios, hack-a-thons, Stanford's D School, and IDEO.

Goleman, Daniel. *Social intelligence: the new science of human relationships*. New York: Bantam Books, 2006.

Thorp, Holden and Buck Goldstein. *Engines of innovation the entrepreneurial university in the twenty-first century*. Chapel Hill: University of North Carolina Press, 2010.

Kuhn, Thomas. *The structure of scientific revolutions*. Chicago: University of Chicago Press, 1970.

Urhahn Urban Design (Firm). *The spontaneous city.* Amsterdam: BIS Publishers, 2011.

Shushok, Frank. "Why didn't I think of that? Dodging big ruts for big ideas in higher education." *About Campus* 18, no. 6 (2014): 30-32.

Crow, Michael and William Dabars. *Designing the new American university.* Baltimore: Johns Hopkins University Press, 2015.

Nielsen, Michael. *Reinventing discovery: the new era of networked science.* Princeton University Press, 2012.

Morville, Peter. "Intertwingled: information changes everything." Ann Arbor, Michigan: Semantic Studios, 2014.

Sculley, John. *Moonshot!: game-changing strategies to build billion-dollar businesses.* New York: RosettaBooks, 2014.

"Radical Collaboration" and being around smart people

Moretti, Enrico. *The new geography of jobs.* Boston: Houghton Mifflin Harcourt, 2012.

Intersections

Johansson, Frans. *The Medici effect: breakthrough insights at the intersection of ideas, concepts, and cultures.* Boston, Mass: Harvard Business School Press, 2004.

Citizenship and democracy

Goldman, Corrie. "Novelist Marilynne Robinson warns Stanford audience against utilitarian trends in higher education." *Stanford University News.* November 3, 2015. Access on November 13, 2015. http://news.stanford.edu/news/2015/november/robinson-humanities-lecture-110315.html